HOMOSEXUALITY
IS DIFFERENT FROM
EATING SHRIMP

WHAT DOES THE BIBLE SAY ABOUT
SEXUALITY AND WHY IS THE CHURCH
SO AFRAID TO TELL YOU?

ALAN FREEMAN

Please contact me if you would like to request a speaking engagement, become a partner, support this ministry with a donation, or any other enquiries.

alanfreemanministries@gmail.com

www.afmi.co.uk

Facebook

https://www.facebook.com/AlanFreemanMinistries/

All scripture references are from the Modern English Version unless otherwise stated.

This book is dedicated to my Lord Jesus Christ, who completed a perfect work at Calvary, that we may have life in all its fullness.

Contents

Forward

By Marybeth Wuenschel
Spirit Filled Catholic

Every Pastor needs to read this book

Every Father

Every Mother

Every Christian

And the sooner, the better.

If you are compromised sexually or doubting your sexuality, this book is for you. If you are fearful, experiencing intrusive thoughts, hearing voices, or seeing things, this book is for you. This book is a great and timely read if you wonder who you are or are supposed to be. It is not for the cowardly or timid. Alan doesn't mince words but exposes the lies of the devil. You have an enemy, and he won't stop till you are destroyed and have turned away from God.

Alan Freeman wants you free. He doesn't want to accuse or condemn you but to free you. He is not afraid to tell the truth because he knows you want the truth. We all want the truth. Jesus said, "You will know the truth, and the truth will set you free." It isn't the truth that sets you free; it is knowing the truth that sets you free. WELL, THAT IS WHAT THIS BOOK IS GOING TO DO FOR YOU; SET YOU FREE from misery, depression, mental illness, and all the devil is hammering you with.

This isn't a beat-yourself-up lecture on what is right or wrong about homosexuality; this is God's love and word for you, and His love speaks through every page.

Every time I hear Alan speak, I make sure I have a pen and paper to take notes. You are going to be treated to a wonderful, no holds barred, sometimes graphic, resource rich book from a man who loves you. If you are a preacher like I am, this book will provide you with the tools you need to coach and counsel not just those who are caught up in sexual sin but those trapped in addictions, depression, and mental illness. We have not been taught how to help those trapped, we were taught to avoid them, exclude them, punish them and deny them hope.

People are suffering and need us. They need us equipped. This book equips us to go where God is leading us armed with the resources we need to powerfully cast out demons, heal the sick and raise the dead to new life.

The devil wants you believing you have gone too far and don't deserve God. He wants you experiencing all that hell has to offer so you won't believe God wants you. God has the answer for whatever you are going through and what he is offering is so much more exciting and rewarding and thrilling than the trap the devil has set. Get free now.

Thank you Alan for the honor of allowing me to share my thoughts and invite my brothers and sisters to dive in.

Forward

By Senior Pastor Rinaldo Olah
Apostolska Cirkev Sabinov

If your life is in a mess and you have no peace and want to change, this book is for you. Within these pages are numerous examples of people who have been set free from their self-destructive lifestyles and who overcame their struggles with shame and guilt. Jesus said, "The thief comes only to steal, kill, and destroy. I came that you may have life and have it more abundantly". The more we sin, the more we become tied up in life. Jesus is the Savior, the Son of the living God, Alpha and Omega, the Beginning and the End, the Bright Morning Star, the One who died for you and rose to life again, who now sits on the right hand of His Father on the throne, who was given all power in heaven and earth. He can save you, deliver you, restore you, turn your life around from despair to peace, so that you become blessed and can then be a blessing to others. Many people struggle, living an unhappy life. Think of a person whose car stops working. They try everything they can to repair it but can't eliminate the problems. Eventually, they decide to take the car back to the manufacturer. The car is then fixed and working as well as new in a short time. So it is with your life. You have tried everything to fix your problems, but things go from bad to worse. This book is your friend because it will point you back to the One who made you, the One who knows you, who understands everything about you, and knows what is needed to fix you up again. This person is Jesus, the One who died for you on the cross. He is the answer you have been looking for. He will lead you from being cursed into being blessed, from self-hatred into love and acceptance. This powerful book will show you the way to freedom and liberty. I urge you to take the time to read it and allow Jesus to turn your life around and give you a new identity.

Romans 13:11-14 TLB

Another reason for right living is this: you know how late it is; time is running out. Wake up, for the coming of the Lord is nearer now than when we first believed. The night is far gone, the day of his return will soon be here. So quit the evil deeds of darkness and put on the armor of right living, as we who live in the daylight should! Be decent and true in everything you do so that all can approve your behavior. Don't spend your time in wild parties and getting drunk or in adultery and lust or fighting or jealousy. But ask the Lord Jesus Christ to help you live as you should, and don't make plans to enjoy evil.

Chapter One

TO EVERYONE WHO IS ANYONE

AND TO ANYONE WHO IS A WHOSOEVER

God loves you.

Whoever you are, whatever you have done, whatever has been done to you, Jesus knows you better than you know yourself and He loves you. You may disagree with Him, feel angry with Him, or be indifferent about Him, but whether you know Him or not, love Him or hate Him, Jesus loves you and wants you. He isn't mad at you, He loves you, and He has the power and the desire to intervene in your life and help you. Jesus is big enough to cope with you. He loves you unconditionally, and there is nothing you can do to change that. This book is a message of hope to those who struggle with homosexuality, as well as other sexual sins, and also for family and friends affected by these issues. Jesus wants to save those who feel lost and set free all who are bound and held captive.

This book is a message of hope to those who struggle with homosexuality.

> ***whosoever shall call on the name of the Lord shall be delivered.***

Joel 2:32

If you are a whosoever, you qualify to receive all the deliverance you need. God wants you to be brave enough to trust Him, to allow Him into your life. Jesus has the power and desire to make you a brand-new person and give you a fresh start in life. He wants to:

- Set you free from tormenting thoughts and feelings.
- Remove your guilt and shame.
- Give you peace and rest.
- Hope and a future.
- Purpose and success.
- Jesus will forgive you so entirely that it will be as though you had never sinned.

God isn't mad at you. He is on your side, and the most significant thing you could ever do for Him is to accept His hand of friendship.

> ***For God did not send his Son into the world to condemn the world, but that the world through Him might be saved.***

John 3:17

Every person has a precious soul that needs saving. Jesus loves you and wants to help you. He did not come to condemn you but to save you.

> ***God anointed Jesus of Nazareth with the Holy Spirit and with power, who went about doing good and healing all***

who were oppressed by the devil, for God was with Him.

Acts 10:38 NKJV

God wants to adopt you as His child so you can be part of the family. He has made a way for everyone to have this close relationship with Him. No matter who you are, what you have done, or what has happened to you. He knows everything about you, yet He loves you and wants you.

Jesus is the only one you can completely trust in, and it would be wise to give yourself to Him.

God is not angry with anyone! He loves you and He has the power and desire to help you.

But God demonstrates His own love toward us, in that while we were yet sinners, Christ died for us.

Romans 5:8

God is loving, merciful, kind, gracious, and good, but He is also holy, righteous, and intolerant of sin. People make the mistake of thinking that He is either one or the other, while He is both at the same time. Jesus demonstrated God's heart towards all sinners in John 8 when a woman who had been caught in adultery was brought before Him.

When Jesus had stood up and saw no one but the Woman, He said to her, "Woman, where are your accusers? Did no one condemn you?" She said, "No one, Lord. "

> ***Jesus said to her, "Neither do I condemn you. Go and sin no more."***
>
> **John 8:10-11**

Jesus didn't just forgive the woman for her sin; He also told her to stop doing it. God's message to everyone who is caught up in sexual sin is the same. God loves you but is intolerant of your sin; He is willing to forgive you, but you must stop doing it.

All sexual activity outside of marriage between a man and a woman is sin.

We love to categorize some sins as being worse than others, but sin is sin. Is homosexuality worse than other sexual sins? It is like comparing a 500-year prison sentence to a 200-year prison sentence. Either way, you are in big trouble. It would be wise to ask the judge for mercy and listen carefully to what He says about your case. We have inherited our sinful status, and as soon as we are able, we all begin to sin ourselves. God, however, in His goodness, has already solved our problem by bearing the punishment we deserved upon Himself when He suffered and died on the cross, which is the most fantastic deal ever. We get all the benefits without any suffering.

Our peace with God was a gift given to us by the Lord Himself. We did nothing to earn it; we do not deserve it, but we get all the benefit of it.

> ***For by grace, you have been saved through faith; and this is not your own doing, it is the gift of God - not because of works, lest any man should boast.***
>
> **Ephesians 2:8-9 RSV**

Our right standing with God is by God's grace alone. We cannot add to it or become even slightly worthy of it. It is the most one-sided deal in the history of deals! It is a gift from God to us.

> ***For the wages of sin is death; but the gift of God is eternal life through Jesus Christ our Lord.***

Romans 6:23 KJV

There are two groups of people in the world: those who have received God's undeserved gift of forgiveness and those who have yet to access His forgiveness.

All sexual activity outside of marriage between a man and a woman is sin.

God's people are Christ's ambassadors in this world, called to share the good news of His salvation with all people. Christians must not be judgmental or self-righteous but rather be a people of love, carrying a goodwill message from a gracious God. We have the secret knowledge of salvation in Christ and eternal punishment for those who refuse Him, and our mission is to rescue as many people as possible from Hell.

God's offer of forgiveness and friendship goes out to anyone and everyone who wants to leave their life of sin.

> ***Listen! I stand at the door and knock. If anyone hears My voice and opens the door, I will come in and dine with him, and he with Me.***

Revelation 3:20

The church has a solemn mission to call all sinners to repentance, and this book will carefully explain how you can overcome the lust of the flesh and become a disciple of Christ.

People who participate in homosexuality must stop doing it, turn away from this lifestyle, and follow the Lord Jesus Christ. A drowning man needs a lifeline. What wicked person would ignore their impending doom and speak of drowning as something to be encouraged and celebrated? So it is with homosexuality. We must do everything possible to warn people and throw them the lifeline of God's love and forgiveness.

Any compromise in this message is treacherous and profoundly unloving.

Chapter Two

UNMASKING THE DEVIL

AND EXPOSING HIS LIES

The enemy is here, and battle is upon us. Satan is coming for you, your children, your family, your church, and your country. He is at work throughout society in education, media, government, and the church.

Jesus is also at work in the world. He loves you so much that He sent me to write this book for you. The devil is trying to silence every voice that disagrees with his rebellious narrative, but if you are reading this book, it shows you that his plan isn't working. Satan is a liar who hates you and wants to destroy you, but God loves you and wants to give you a prosperous future.

Homosexuals are precious people who have fallen into sin. The sin can be dealt with and removed.

God defines sexual sin in the Bible, and He will judge all those who live rebellious lifestyles against His ways. God loves every person who is homosexual, but He hates their homosexuality.

> ***There is a way that seems right to a man, but its end is the way to death.***
>
> **Proverbs 16:25 RSV**

The principles and concepts I am sharing are not mere theories; they have been tried and tested over many years of pastoral ministry and will set you free from the entrapment of sexual sin.

I will not be using the term "gay" to describe homosexuality, nor will I be using LGBTQIA+ to refer to people who are made in the image of God.

Homosexuals are precious people who have fallen into sin. The sin can be dealt with and removed.

Using the term homosexual to describe those who have same-sex relations is perfectly correct. It should not be considered offensive, but in my experience, using the term homosexual is often viewed negatively. Why is this so? I believe there is a descriptive nature to the word homosexual that makes people feel uncomfortable. Using the term "gay" is an attempt to hide its true nature and cast a veneer of decency over this lifestyle.

Society presents homosexuality as something good and wholesome, while in reality, it is sordid and shameful.

Homosexuality is unnatural, unclean, unholy, and unacceptable to the Lord.

Some argue that homosexuality is natural and God-given because we are all made in His image. They teach that a homosexual is entitled to gratify their sexual desires just as much as a heterosexual person. The Bible, however, states that you need to deny yourself and serve the law of God in all that you do.

And he said to them all, if any man will come after me, let him deny himself, and take up his cross daily, and follow me.

Luke 9:23 KJV

If something in your life is contrary to God's Word, it must be denied.

Morality is not subjective. It is not based on what you want, or on what seems reasonable to you, or on culture, or contemporary thinking. God Himself objectively establishes morality. Jesus is the one who sets the moral compass in all things. His Word is final. God does not change His mind to fit in with us. We need to change our minds to fit in with Him.

The church has often failed to help those who are lost in sin. They have fallen into the trap of either self-righteously condemning people or betraying them with a liberal theology.

The entirety of Your word is truth, and every one of Your righteous judgments endures forever.

Psalm 119:160

The church has often failed to help those who are lost in sin. They have fallen into the trap of either self-righteously condemning people or betraying them with a liberal theology.

The gospel of repentance must be preached with compassion for the listeners. Real problems need real help. Jesus wants everyone to come to Him and receive His forgiveness, and

He wants His church to be skilled in healing those who struggle with sinful lifestyles.

> ***They have healed also the hurt of the daughter of my people slightly, saying, Peace, peace, when there is no peace.***

Jeremiah 6:14 KJV

Homosexuals have been judged, shunned, or appeased by the church but rarely loved, which is not pleasing to the Lord.

Love does not condemn, but neither does it avoid telling the truth. Jesus suffered and died on the cross so that everyone can receive all the forgiveness, healing, and restoration they need. Some people will view this book as hateful and homophobic, which I strongly disagree with.

It would be hateful and homophobic NOT to tell you how God views homosexuality.

Chapter Three

HOODWINKED

DEVLISH LIES AND SATANIC STRATEGIES

Satan is the enemy of the state. Successful societies are established with reverence for the Lord Jesus Christ and His book, the Bible. The greatness of America and other countries came about because they were founded on biblical truth and the fear of the Lord. Satan is trying to destroy our society by supplanting godly order with his own rebellious agenda.

> ***The thief's purpose is to steal, kill and destroy. My purpose is to give life in all its fullness.***
>
> **John 10:10 TLB**

The devil works through people, and he used Alice Bailey to develop the New Age Movement. Alice Bailey was an occultist who received these teachings directly from a demon spirit guide called Djual Khul. This evil woman was promoting these ideas over a hundred years ago. Here is an example of the instructions given to her.

Alice Bailey's Ten Point Charter to Destroy Christianity

1. Take God and prayer out of the education system.
2. Reduce parental authority over the children.
3. Destroy the Judeo-Christian family structure or the traditional Christian family structure.
4. If sex is free, then make abortion legal and make it easy.
5. Make divorce easy and legal, free people from the concept of marriage for life.
6. Make homosexuality an alternative lifestyle.
7. Debase art, make it run mad.
8. Use media to promote and change mindsets.
9. Create an interfaith movement.
10. Get governments to make these laws and get the church to endorse these changes.

This ten-point charter reveals Satan's strategic attack against the peoples of the world, and unfortunately, these satanic teachings have been embraced throughout society and the church. Making homosexuality a valid lifestyle alters people's sense of right and wrong and corrupts their moral compass.

Satan wants to change the foundations upon which the individual, the family, the church, and the nation are built.

He is using homosexuality to do this as he works to turn the hearts and minds of people against God and all that is healthy, noble, and good. Homosexuality is now a protected right, as is abortion, and pedophilia will soon follow. Satan is perverting people's sense of right and wrong

You can serve the devil, or you can serve the Lord Jesus Christ, but you cannot serve both.

and searing their conscience so that when his Anti-Christ is unveiled, he will be instantly welcomed and followed.

> ***Woe to those who call evil good, and good evil; who exchange darkness for light, and light for darkness; who exchange bitter for sweet, and sweet for bitter!***
>
> **Isaiah 5:20**

If people cannot discern that homosexuality is wrong, how will they be able to discern that the Anti-Christ is of the devil? Falling for the lie that men can become women and women men is a sure sign that the world is ready for the Man of Lawlessness to be revealed.

> ***The coming of the lawless one is according to the working of Satan, with all power, signs, and lying wonders, and with all unrighteous deception among those who perish because they did not receive the love of the truth, that they might be saved. And for this reason, God will send them strong delusion, that they should believe the lie, that they all may be condemned who did not believe the truth but had pleasure in unrighteousness.***
>
> **2 Thessalonians 2:9-12**

Satan has only one problem - the faithful followers of the Lord Jesus Christ. Loving truth is a protection from deception. Those who do not love the truth are vulnerable to deception and become the enemies of God.

You can serve the devil, or you can serve the Lord Jesus Christ, but you cannot serve both. There are only two options and thinking you can choose neither automatically casts you in the devil's camp.

> ***(Jesus said) "He who is not with Me is against Me, and he who does not gather with Me scatters."***

Luke 11:23 RSV

God is not a liar. He is all-powerful, Almighty, maker of heaven and earth, of all that is, seen and unseen. God always tells the truth, and He is so sure about His Words that He put them in His book, the Bible. God is the author of the scriptures, and He has carefully watched over the Bible to preserve it as a faithful account of His Words.

> ***First of all, you must understand this, that no prophecy of scripture is a matter of one's own interpretation, because no prophecy ever came by the impulse of man, but men moved by the Holy Spirit spoke from God.***

2 Peter 1:20-21 RSV

Satan knows that the Bible is absolute truth and the final authority on all matters.

His success in your life depends upon how much he can keep this knowledge from you.

Chapter Four

WOLVES IN WOLVES CLOTHING

THE OPEN APOSTASY OF FALSE TEACHERS AND LYING LEADERS

Dreadful wolves will enter among you, not sparing the flock. Even from among you men will arise speaking perverse things, to draw the disciples away after them.

Acts 20:29-30

There are many today who teach that homosexuality is not a sin. False teachers in the church are spreading such lies, attempting to deceive all who listen to them. Forsaking the truth of God's ways and scorning the Bible, they redefine righteousness according to their own wisdom. They have created an imaginary god who allows them to follow their own foolish ideas, but their god has no power because he doesn't actually exist.

> ***But there were false prophets, too, in those days, just as there will be false teachers among you. They will cleverly tell their lies about God, turning against even their Master who bought them; but theirs will be a swift and terrible end. Many will follow their evil teaching that there is nothing wrong with sexual sin. And because of them Christ and his way will be scoffed at.***

2 Peter 2:1-2 TLB

Many Bishops, Priests, and Church Leaders throughout the denominations have now reneged on the foundational doctrines of Christianity. In the past, there have been some ungodly leaders, but never before in the history of the church has there been such open apostasy, such public abandonment of the basic tenets of the faith.

> ***For my people have committed two evils; they have forsaken me the fountain of living waters, and hewed them out cisterns, broken cisterns, that can hold no water.***

Jerimiah 2:13 KJV

These spiritually bankrupt leaders promote a gospel of grace without repentance and love without holiness. Claiming to represent God, these wolves in wolves clothing teach that homosexuality is something good that should be celebrated and blessed. Many Archbishops and denominational leaders have rejected the Bible as God's Word. No longer considering scripture to be the final authority on all matters, they have turned to human reason and cultural trends to give them direction and guidance for their moral compass.

These ungodly leaders are now commissioning others like themselves into the church to teach and pastor God's people. How many have been discouraged and led astray by these servants of the devil? How many are blinded to the gospel of salvation by these false teachers?

> ***Then the Lord said, "These prophets are telling lies in my name. I did not send them or tell them to speak. I did not give them any messages. They prophesy of visions and revelations they have never seen or heard. They speak foolishness made up in their own lying hearts.***

Jeremiah 14:14 NLT

Such leaders do not represent the Lord Jesus Christ. They have elevated their own ideas above the wisdom of God, choosing the praise of men over the fear of the Lord.

> ***"Why do you call Me, 'Lord, Lord,' and not do what I say?"***

Luke 6:46

These spiritual charlatans have despised the first commandment, which is to love the Lord your God with all your heart, soul, and mind, and then disobeyed the second commandment by betraying their neighbors with lies and falsehoods.

These devilish imposters are not fit to be leaders in the body of Christ; they are a fifth column of wickedness in God's church.

Their refusal to speak about the sin of homosexuality is treacherous and profoundly unloving, as it denies people the opportunity to repent and be healed from this lifestyle.

> ***Whoever causes one of these little ones who believe in Me to sin, it would be better for him if a millstone were hung around his neck, and he were thrown into the sea. If your hand causes you to sin, cut it off. It is better for you to enter life maimed than with two hands to go into hell, into the fire that shall never be quenched, where: 'their worm does not die, and the fire is not quenched.'***

Mark 9:42-44

Such leaders do not represent the Lord Jesus Christ. They have elevated their own ideas above the wisdom of God, choosing the praise of men over the fear of the Lord.

A gospel of grace without repentance and love without the cross has no power to save. It is worthless religion and offensive to God. These lying leaders and false teachers have brought the church into disrepute. Their stance is pleasing to men but offensive to the Lord. Blessing that which is an abomination is denying Christ and leading people into sin.

> ***Woe to those who call evil good, and good evil; who exchange darkness for light, and light for darkness; who exchange bitter for sweet, and sweet for bitter!***
>
> **Isaiah 5:20**

God loves each one of us, but there will be eternal consequences to our lifestyle choices. The Bible is clear that homosexuality is entirely unacceptable to God. The good news is that God has the power and the desire to forgive this sin and heal this perversion.

> ***If my people, which are called by my name, shall humble themselves, and pray, and seek my face, and turn from their wicked ways; then will I hear from heaven, and will forgive their sin, and will heal their land.***
>
> **2 Chronicles 7:14 KJV**

Blessing that which is an abomination is denying Christ and leading people into sin.

The most loving thing a Christian can do is to warn people that they will soon be held accountable to the Lord Jesus Christ. On that fearful day when we will all stand before Him, it will only be His opinion that matters. All other reasoning, words, arguments, and pleadings will count for nothing. You can choose to trust in man's wisdom or the Word of God.

Choose wisely. Your eternal destiny depends on it.

Chapter Five

HOMOSEXUALITY

THE WAY IN

You shall not lie with a man as one does with a woman. It is an abomination.

Leviticus 18:22

God did not create anyone to be homosexual. He has never made anything that is forbidden in His Word. During their life, some people become homosexual, while others mistakenly feel that they have always been so. Same-sex attraction is not natural. It can come about in several ways, including molestation, sex outside of marriage, pornography, and generational inheritance.

MOLESTATION

If a person is attacked and sexually abused, they have done nothing wrong, but demons can still be transferred from the attacker into the victim. The assault is always both physical and spiritual. During sex, even if it isn't penetrative, a link or tie is established between the two people. Their physical bodies and souls open up to each other, and demons can pass from one person to the other. In sexual abuse, there will always be demons of abuse and lust present, and often demons of homosexuality and pedophilia, amongst others.

Do you not know that he who is joined to a harlot is one body with her? For "the two," He says, "shall become one flesh."

1 Corinthians 6:16

'For this cause shall a man leave his father and mother, and cleave to his wife, and the two shall be one flesh.' So, then they are no longer two, but one flesh.

Mark 10:7-8

Satan is always seeking to place demons inside of people, and one of the quickest ways of doing this is through sexual misconduct or molestation. The devil hates children and always seeks to hurt them with sexual molestation. He also targets children so that demons can get access and have a lifetime of opportunity to work in and through them.

The demons will begin to torment the person with intrusive thoughts and feelings, including unwanted sexual feelings and desires, trauma, nightmares, low self-worth, fear, and anxiety. These symptoms will significantly reduce once we follow a godly pathway of forgiving the abuser and then driving out all demons that came into you through the attack.

PLEASE NOTE, forgiveness does not mean that you shouldn't report the abuser to the authorities. The Christian should always forgive people, but you must ensure that the person is brought to justice and punished with the full force of the law, and forgiveness does NOT necessarily mean you should remain in relationship with the person.

SEX OUTSIDE OF MARRIAGE

Sex between a man and a woman in marriage is blessed and protected.

> ***Marriage is to be honoured among everyone, and the bed undefiled. But God will judge the sexually immoral and adulterers.***
>
> **Hebrews 13:4**

Sex outside of godly marriage does not have the same blessings and protection, and demons can pass from one person to another. The most extensive sexually transmitted disease is not Chlamydia; it is demons. The Bible tells us to flee from sexual sin.

> ***Flee sexual immorality. Every sin that a man does is outside the body, but he who commits sexual immorality sins against his own body.***
>
> **1 Corinthians 6:18 NKJV**

Sex between two people outside of marriage is so dangerous. Not only is it a sin, but you do not know what demons the person has inside of them. After having sex, you may find that you suddenly have a new desire for something you never felt before. If the other person has a demon of homosexuality in them and the demon decides to enter you, for the first time in your life, you will

> ***Satan is a strategist who will target Christians and bring people into their lives to seduce them into sexual sin.***

start having feelings of same-sex attraction and a lust for this sin.

Each demon is associated with a particular behavior, such as lust, anger, sickness, fear, etc. If, for instance, the person had a demon of epilepsy and it decided to transfer into you, epileptic fits will begin to happen in your life. The doctors can medicate you to help with the illness, but the underlying issue won't disappear until the demon is cast out.

Demons don't necessarily have to pass from one person to another. They may feel more comfortable in the person they are with. But if a Christian becomes available, they will most likely transfer into them so that they can afflict them and hinder their effectiveness against their master's kingdom.

The transfer of demons is a huge reason to flee from sexual sin!

Satan is a strategist who will target Christians and bring people into their lives to seduce them into sexual sin. He does this to place demons into the person and create problems in their lives. Suppose you suddenly find that you are receiving a lot of attention from someone. In that case, it may not be because they see you as attractive and desirable; it may be that the demons in them are stirring up lustful feelings towards you in the hope that you will be stupid enough to commit sexual sin with their host. They can then breach your defenses and flood into you.

King Solomon was a classic example of a God-fearing man who fell into sexual sin, child sacrifice, and demon worship. The Lord warned him not to marry wives from ungodly nations, and the reason for this was that these women were infested with demons. He didn't listen and became inhabited by these demons himself.

> ***But King Solomon loved many foreign women in addition to the daughter of Pharaoh, women of the Moabites, Ammonites, Edomites, Sidonians, and Hittites, from the nations which the Lord warned the children of Israel about, saying, "You shall not go into them, nor shall they come into you, for they will surely turn your heart away toward their gods."***

1 Kings 11:1-2

> ***"For Solomon went after Ashtoreth the goddess of the Sidonians, and after Milcom the abomination of the Ammonites."***

1 Kings 11:5

The gods of these nations were demon spirits who motivated the people to practice every kind of wickedness possible. When Solomon disobeyed the Lord and had sex with the women from these nations, the demons in them could pass into him. These demons began to pollute his thinking, stirring up thoughts of sexual immorality and sinful activity, and inevitably, he eventually fell away from the Lord.

The transfer of demons is a huge reason to flee from sexual sin!

In witchcraft and Satanism, some men and women are chosen to be inhabited by demons of seduction. These servants of the devil are sent to have sex with selected people so that demons can be transferred into them. These carriers of demons are placed into churches and sent against Christians, especially leaders, to entice them into having sex. The demons are passed into the people, who then find they become consumed with lust and desire more sex with the Satanist and other people. This is also done to draw people into the coven or the Satanist group. Christians are frequently targeted so that their marriages and ministries are destroyed.

These Satanists in the church will look like perfectly respectable Christians, and we need to be sensitive to the Holy Spirit to discern their hidden intentions. Churches need solid policies and procedures about how men and women work with members of the opposite sex. Married people should not spend time alone with someone of the opposite sex who isn't their spouse, to protect them from temptation and also from false accusations.

Children's activities in church must follow strict safeguarding policies to ensure that pedophiles cannot gain access to children. Pedophiles, homosexuals, and transgenders who visit church need to hear the gospel of repentance so that they can leave their life of sin. They can be welcomed, but must be carefully monitored to keep everyone safe, and they must NEVER be left alone with children or vulnerable people.

We are to love everyone coming to our churches, but we must keep people safe from those with evil intentions. I know of churches that the infiltration of witches has destroyed, but also churches that were wise to such people, and the witches ended up repenting and coming to Christ.

Sexual sin is the gateway to destruction.

Satanists will sometimes present as decent, upstanding citizens, but their goal is to destroy Christian marriages, molest your children, and devastate churches.

> ***For such are false apostles and deceitful workers, disguising themselves as apostles of Christ. And no wonder! For even Satan disguises himself as an angel of light. Therefore, it is no great thing if his ministers also disguise themselves as ministers of righteousness, whose end will be according to their works.***
>
> **2 Corinthians 11:13-15**

> ***Be sober and watchful, because your adversary the devil walks around as a roaring lion, seeking whom he may devour.***
>
> **1 Peter 5:8**

> ***lest Satan should get an advantage of us. For we are not ignorant of his devices.***
>
> **2 Corinthians 2:11 KJV**

> ***Beloved, believe not every spirit, but try the spirits whether they are of God: because many false prophets are gone out into the world.***
>
> **1 John 4:1 KJV**

Sexual sin is the gateway to destruction.

I knew a minister that was happily married with a promising ministry. He lived with his family in an area where many prostitutes plied their trade, and unfortunately, he fell into sin with one of them. I presume he had tried witnessing to her, but he was foolish to do so without prayer support and someone accompanying him. He didn't lead her to Christ, but she led him into sexual sin, and his life fell apart. He developed a lust for prostitutes; then, he began an affair with the worship leader in the church. Despite the efforts of his loving wife and his church, he became consumed with sexual immorality, and he ended up out of the ministry. The last time I saw him, he was mentally and physically in a bad way. I believe the devil targeted him, and he fell into sin through a lack of wisdom and accountability. Demons of prostitution and lust entered him, along with God only knows what other demons, and he found himself unable to leave his life of sin. The demons that tempted him from the outside were now living inside him, and their influence was many times greater than it was when they were on the outside.

God has provided everything needed to be healed and restored from sin, but if we don't know how to minister correctly, the devil will prevail against us and destroy our lives. After sinning, this minister needed to confess his sin, stop doing it, share his failings with those he was accountable to, and then take authority and expel every demon placed into him through his sinful behavior. He then needed to accept the consequences of his actions, leave the ministry, and submit to the care and direction of godly elders until God could restore him. Sadly, he was unwilling to do so, and his life is in ruins today. The verse Hosea 4:6 is so true.

> ***My people are destroyed for lack of knowledge.***
>
> **Hosea 4:6 KJV**

I worked with another man who felt that sometimes he was a man and sometimes a woman. He was promiscuous and would have sex with men and also have sex with women prostitutes. One day, he would dress as a woman; other times, he would be a man, but often he was something in between. He explained that he liked to dress as a man but wore makeup and women's underwear. He showed no interest in the gospel, and our paths soon parted, but I thought about him having sex with prostitutes. This man had demons of homosexuality and transgenderism in him, and who knows what others. He would regularly be with hookers, and the demons in him would be able to pass into them, then the next customer who came along could become infested with demons of homosexuality, etc. Prostitutes have many demons in them, and demons are allowed to pass into other people through them. I knew of a Christian who visited a prostitute and was never the same afterward. He repented of his sin but didn't understand about deliverance. From that time onwards, there was an uncleanness about him, which caused much rejection. He became a proud person and quite unteachable. I have seen this trait in other Christians who needed deliverance. They have been involved in sexual sin and repented, but they refused to consider that they would have allowed demons into them and laughed at the idea that they needed deliverance. I believe that pride is a primary influence of demons in a person.

> ***A one-minute prayer could change the whole course of a person's life and save them from many troubles.***

PORNOGRAPHY

This is discussed at length in Chapter Seven.

GENERATIONAL INHERITANCE

> ***The Lord is slow to anger and abounding in mercy, forgiving iniquity and transgression; but He will by no means clear the guilty, visiting the iniquity of the fathers upon the children to the third and fourth generation.***

Numbers 14:18

Some people claim that they were born homosexual. I believe that this can appear to be the case, but it is not because homosexuality is something natural and normal; it is because the person inherited a demon of homosexuality, even while they were in the womb. I would also say that some people can receive demons as babies without spiritual awareness and protection in their homes. When a demon enters a person, it will stay there until it is either driven out or the person dies. When they die, their demons can pass to another family member or close relative as part of their inheritance. We need to pray and cleanse our family lines from spiritual inheritance.

> ***My people are gone into captivity because they have no knowledge.***

Isaiah 5:13 KJV

We need to cleanse our family lines by saying a simple prayer and taking authority over any demons who have the right to afflict us generationally.

A one-minute prayer could change the whole course of a person's life and save them from many troubles.

I have witnessed this happening, where demons passed from an elderly aunt into her young niece. The aunt was a person of anger and strife who used to threaten and dominate the people around her, even becoming violent if someone opposed her. When she died, her niece had a sudden personality change and developed the same characteristics as her aunt. The difference in the girl was startling, and she even began to have the same facial expressions and way of speaking that her aunt had. She began to bully and intimidate the people in her life, even physically attacking one of her uncles in the same way as her aunt used to do.

A glaring example of a generational curse and how demons can enter a family line is found in 2 Samuel chapters 11-18. King David committed adultery with Bathsheba, then murdered her husband to cover up his sin. Demons of sexual immorality and murder entered him and his family line. From this time onward, sexual sin and bloodshed recurred from generation to generation. King David's son Amnon raped his sister Tamar, Absalom murdered Amnon, Absalom raped King David's concubines on a rooftop, Absalom was murdered, King Solomon became a sex addict, and so on. Praise God that our sins are forgiven on this side of the cross, and demons can be driven out in Jesus' name. For further reading, see Chapter 14 on deliverance. I include this passage from the Chapter.

> ***Sometimes, demons pass through the family line. If you suspect this may be the case, tell the Lord about the sins committed by your forefathers and mothers, and ask the Lord to cleanse***

your family lines in Jesus' name. With each suspected area of your family where you think demons may be able to inhabit, ask the Lord to block any demons from continuing to travel through the mechanism of inheritance. Again, speak out loud and command all demons that passed through the generations to get out of you and leave your family forever. Ask the Lord to seal you and your immediate family from all demonic inheritance.

Chapter 14

The devil is brutalizing people, destroying their sense of right and wrong, casting confusion over their discernment, and making them vulnerable to everything he wants to do in their lives.

The devil is using the music industry, the internet, media, movies, books, fashion, education, and even the church to influence us toward sexual sin.

Satan is mobilizing his forces against society, using such things as homosexuality, transgenderism, free sex, pornography, pedophilia, and child sacrifice (abortion).

Satan hates everyone, including those who knowingly serve him. He aggressively promotes homosexuality because he hates God and wants to desecrate his creation. Homosexuality destroys life. Same-sex relationships produce no offspring, so the more people he perverts, the less people will be born into the world.

The devil is strategically targeting our young people. Our education system is coming under the influence of demons, even in the so-called Christian schools and colleges. From kindergarten to university, our young people are being indoctrinated with ideas contrary to the scriptures. Children are embracing homosexuality and transgenderism, with many of them remaining childless as a result. Those who become pregnant are encouraged to murder their child in the abortion clinic. Men see themselves as women; women, men, and others say they are neither. Our young people are under the most horrific attack ever seen on the face of the planet in an attempt to create a whole generation that hates Jesus Christ and His ways, being encouraged to despise everything good and wholesome, calling evil good, and losing their discernment over right and wrong.

> ***Now the Spirit clearly says that in the last times some will depart from the faith and pay attention to seducing spirits and doctrines of devils, speaking lies in hypocrisy, having their consciences seared with a hot iron.***

1 Timothy 4:1-2

The devil is using the music industry, the internet, media, movies, books, fashion, education, and even the church to influence us toward sexual sin.

He is the force behind the belief that we need to indulge every thought and feeling, no matter how evil or damaging they are to us. Our battle is not against people; it is against the devil and his demons. Every person we meet has a precious soul that needs saving. Our fight is against the enemy of humanity, the devil himself.

For we wrestle not against flesh and blood, but against principalities, against powers, against the rulers of the darkness of this world, against spiritual wickedness in high places.

Ephesians 6:12 KJV

Satan is on the move, and he's coming for you.

He wants your children, marriage, church, and country. Christians need to stop being passive to the devil's mischief and begin making a stand for righteousness. We are the light in this world, and as the darkness intensifies, we must align ourselves with the Lord Jesus Christ and shine out like a lighthouse, illuminating the way so that others can also find salvation and eternal life.

Chapter Six

HOMOSEXUALITY

THE WAY OUT

They shall teach My people the difference between the holy and profane and cause them to discern between the unclean and the clean.

Ezekial 44:23 KJV

People coming out of homosexuality need real help, not just to be told to repent.

Homosexuals need extensive healing and restoration to achieve freedom and victory over same-sex attraction. The cross of Christ provides all that anyone will ever need, but you must help people to access God's healing power. They must join a good church where they will be loved, mentored, and instructed correctly in the truth of God's Word. The church should not be a place of condemnation and self-righteousness, nor somewhere that entertains liberal compromise, but a house of love and truth, where the broken and wounded can receive healing and restoration.

People coming out of homosexuality need real help, not just to be told to repent.

We need to learn to care for people and not be judgmental or look down on those coming from a sinful lifestyle. Let us bear with one another and help to carry each other's burdens. People become severely damaged by homosexuality and need extensive healing after leaving this lifestyle. This passage from Romans gives us an insight into how humans degenerate when they rebel against the Lord in this way.

> ***God gave them up to uncleanness through the lusts of their hearts, to dishonor their own bodies among themselves. They turned the truth of God into a lie and worshipped and served the creature rather than the Creator, who is blessed forever. Amen. For this reason God gave them up to dishonorable passions. Their women exchanged the natural function for what is against nature. Likewise the men, leaving the natural function of the Woman, burned in their lust toward one another, men with men doing that which is shameful, and receiving in themselves the due penalty of their error. And since they did not see fit to acknowledge God, God gave them over to a debased mind, to do those things which are not proper.***

Romans 1:24-28

Homosexuality is a consequence of people who turn away from the Lord and rebel against His ways by refusing to control the lust of their flesh. Homosexuality is an abomination to the Lord and brings judgment to those involved in this wickedness. Fornication with the opposite sex is a sin, but homosexuality is not only sinful; it also severely damages a person, so they must be literally remade as part of their restoration process. The very mind, body and soul of a homosexual becomes degraded and debased.

Only Jesus can heal and restore you, and he is willing to do so. Ask God to re-make your mind and body and give you new desires.

> ***Delight yourself in the Lord, and He will give you the desires of your heart. Commit your way to the Lord; trust also in Him, and He will bring it to pass. He will bring forth your righteousness as the light, and your judgment as the noonday.***
>
> **Psalm 37:4-5**

God promises us that when we look to Him for all we need, He will put new desires into our hearts, replacing the old lusts and cravings. We will begin to have different desires from before, and then the Lord will delight in giving us these new things. Where you once craved same-sex relations, you will now desire the opposite sex. Where you used to lust for drugs, multiple partners, and sexual highs, you will begin to want peace, love, purity, and the fulfilment of a godly marriage. Make Jesus the delight of your heart. Spend time with Him and His Word. Avoid things that oppose Him,

The church should not be a place of condemnation and self-righteousness, nor somewhere that entertains liberal compromise, but a house of love and truth, where the broken and wounded can receive healing and restoration.

such as certain music, performers, or movies. Jesus loves you, so make Him the love of your life.

> ***I made a covenant with my eyes not to look with lust upon a girl.***

Job 31:1 TLB

You go where you're looking.

Look to Jesus. Keep your eyes fixed on Him and His Word. Get to Know Him, walk and talk with Him night and day. Be in constant fellowship with Him.

> ***If you are willing and obedient, you shall eat the good of the land.***

Isaiah 1:19 RSV

God loves you so much, and He wants to take care of you and restore all that you have lost and much more.

> ***You will keep him in perfect peace, whose mind is stayed on You, because he trusts in You. Trust in the Lord forever, for in God the Lord we have an everlasting rock.***

Isaiah 26:3-4

You go where you're looking.

Spend time each day speaking health and healing over yourself. Do this aloud as a prophetic act, declaring the truth over yourself as a statement of fact. For example, say out loud, "I am forgiven of all sin!" I am a new creation in Christ Jesus!"

For God did not send His Son into the world to condemn the world, but that the world through Him might be saved.

John 3:17

I recommend a book called "Prayer Companion" by Marybeth Wuenschel, which has many powerful prayers and declarations you can use.

But godliness with contentment is great gain.

1 Timothy 6:6 KJV

Jesus loves you and wants to help you. He isn't angry with you. He knows your pain and everything that has ever happened to you. He cares about you and wants you to prosper in every area of your life.

For all have sinned and come short of the glory of God.

Romans 3:23 KJV

We have all sinned and fallen short of God's standards, but God will forgive and restore us. Jesus demonstrated His compassion for us when He spoke to the Woman who had been caught committing adultery.

He knows your pain and everything that has ever happened to you. He cares about you and wants you to prosper in every area of your life.

So when they continued asking Him, He stood up and said to them, "Let him who is without sin among you be the first to throw a stone at her." Again He stooped down and wrote on the ground. Being convicted by their conscience, those who heard it went out one by one, beginning with the eldest even to the last. Jesus was left alone, and the Woman standing in the midst. When Jesus had stood up and saw no one but the Woman, He said to her, "Woman, where are your accusers? Did no one condemn you?" She said, "No one, Lord." Jesus said to her, "Neither do I condemn you. Go and sin no more."

John 8:7-11

When Jesus addressed the Woman, He demonstrated the Father's heart towards all sinners. God does not condemn you; He loves you, but you need to stop sinning and receive the forgiveness that Jesus died to obtain for you.

You are not powerless over your sexual orientation and desires. Fight back against the devil and sin!

"Go, and sin no more."

You are not powerless over your sexual orientation and desires. Fight back against the devil and sin!

Submit yourselves to God. Resist the devil, and he will flee from you.

James 4:7

The Lord will heal you and give you your life back. Consider the following actions to take in your life.

- Become a student of God's Word.
- Come into agreement with the Lord about your lifestyle.
- Decide to stop living in sin and ask God to forgive you.
- Command all demons that came into you to leave in Jesus' name.
- Ask the Lord to re-make your heart and mind.
- Get involved with a godly church and become accountable to mature and stable Christians.
- Avoid situations that trigger you, which may mean breaking off friendships and avoiding certain meeting places associated with ungodliness. Change what you watch on screen. Maybe take a break from Facebook and other media and music.
- Use the gift of speaking in tongues daily. See the appendix at the end of the book on how to receive this spiritual gift.

Speaking in tongues is God's secret weapon to restore and heal your body, mind, and soul. Speaking in tongues is a key to recovery from many disorders in life and will transform your relationship with Jesus.

He who speaks in an unknown tongue edifies himself.

1 Corinthians 14:4

The word edify means "To improve someone's mind." Praying in tongues heals wounds that demons leave behind in your body and soul, restoring and improving your mind.

For someone coming out of sexual sin, especially homosexuality, and also things such as the occult, speaking in tongues is essential.

Use the gift privately every day. I recommend speaking in tongues for at least two hours a day, although some people will need to use their gift more than this. Speaking in tongues can be done while driving or doing other activities. Go for a walk while listening to a sermon and speaking in tongues; this will benefit your body, mind, and soul. Speaking in tongues will also help you with reading and understanding the Bible. I cannot recommend this gift too highly.

> ***Why do you spend money for that which is not bread, and your labor for that which does not satisfy? Listen diligently to Me, and eat what is good, and let your soul delight itself in abundance.***

Isaiah 55:2

God wants you to come to Him so that He can bless you. Leaving homosexuality or other sexual sins is never easy, but the Lord will help you every step of the way. Your sin may be big, but Jesus is bigger. He loves you and will heal you completely.

> ***Whoever calls upon the name of the Lord shall be delivered.***

Joel 2:32 KJV

The things of God only work when we do them His way.

You will receive your deliverance once you meet God's conditions. Do not compromise with sin. A little sin will allow the devil a place in your life again, which is a problem you don't need. Study the life of King Saul. He decided to interpret God's commands and mix a little of his wisdom with the Word of God, which cost him everything. Samuel the prophet likened his behavior to rebellion and witchcraft.

For someone coming out of sexual sin, especially homosexuality, and also things such as the occult, speaking in tongues is essential.

> ***Does the Lord delight in burnt offerings and sacrifices as much as in obeying the voice of the Lord? Obedience is better than sacrifice, a listening ear than the fat of rams. For rebellion is as the sin of witchcraft, and stubbornness is as iniquity and idolatry.***

1 Samuel 15:22-23

Be vigilant in keeping control of your mind. Remember that sin begins with a single thought. The example of Samson is a warning. As a Nazirite, Samson could not eat grapes or drink wine, which he obeyed, but when he travelled to Timnah, he walked next to the vineyards.

> ***Samson went down with his father and mother to Timnah. As they came to the vineyards of Timnah, suddenly a young lion came roaring toward him.***

Judges 14:5

Samson was not disobeying the Lord by walking past a vineyard, but he was too close to sin. The Lord sent a lion to attack him as a warning that he was too close to forbidden things. Samson didn't eat the grapes but looked at them, could smell them, and no doubt wondered what it would be like to eat the forbidden fruit. Samson's strength and power depended on his obedience to his Nazirite calling, and when the day came when he finally succumbed to sin, he was bound in chains and had his eyes gouged out.

God still loved him, and the Lord brought him back, but the cost of sinning was terrible for Samson.

When coming out of lifestyles such as homosexuality, you must submit to the Lord and His ways carefully and entirely. Jesus tells you today, "Come follow Me if you want to live." Jesus is the Way - the only way to life. There is no other way for you. It would help to change many old habits and friendships and carefully consider where you hang out. Ask yourself this question. "What business do I have in this place or with these people?" If you are sharing the gospel with lost souls, that is good, but if they don't want your message, leave and try somewhere else.

Meditate on these verses from Proverbs:

> ***Trust in the Lord with all your heart and lean not on your own understanding. In all your ways acknowledge Him, and He will direct your paths. Do not be wise in your own eyes; fear the Lord and depart from evil. It will be health to your body, and strength to your bones.***

Proverbs 3:5-8

Trusting in God rather than yourself is vital if you consider interpreting God's Word to suit your thoughts and feelings. It is good to read this passage in the Amplified Version as well.

> ***Trust in and rely confidently on the Lord with all your heart And do not rely on your own insight or understanding. In all your ways know and acknowledge and recognize Him, And He will make your paths straight and smooth [removing obstacles that block your way]. Do not be wise in your own eyes; Fear the Lord [with reverent awe and obedience] and turn [entirely] away from evil. It will be health to your body [your marrow, your nerves, your sinews, your muscles—all your inner parts] And refreshment (physical well-being) to your bones.***

Proverbs 3:5-8 AMP

The things of God only work when we do them His way.

Be careful to turn away from evil ENTIRELY. Guard your eyes and ears and monitor all the input you receive. If being in a particular place leads you back to sin, don't go there again. I know of a recovering alcoholic who stayed sober all week until he went to visit his friends in the bar. He started the evening with soda, but he was drinking whisky by the end of the night. The solution for him was to stay away from the bar and make new friends.

> ***Seek the Lord while He may be found, call you upon Him while He is near.***

Let the wicked forsake his way, and the unrighteous man his thoughts; and let him return to the Lord, and He will have mercy upon him, and to our God, for He will abundantly pardon.

Isaiah 55:6-7

I heard a testimony from someone who was being severely tempted to buy pornography from a sex shop. He received prayer but was also advised to walk a different route home from work to avoid passing by the shop. He resisted the devil in several ways. He shared his struggle with a brother, commanded demons of lust to leave him, and avoided walking past the place of temptation. He now lives in victory over this sin, praise God!

Be careful to turn away from evil ENTIRELY.

Chapter Seven

PORNOGRAPHY AND SEXUAL FANTASY

THE GATEWAY TO HOMOSEXUALITY AND PEDOPHILIA

I will walk within my house with a perfect heart. I will set no wicked thing before my eyes.

Psalm 101:2-3

Satan uses pornography to gain access to your life. When you access pornography you open a portal from the spirit realm directly into your body, mind, and soul. Underneath the alluring façade of porn are hiding cruel, horrible demons just waiting to jump into you. These demons hate you; their objective is to steal, kill and destroy you, and they gloat over the pain, suffering and misery unfolding in your life. God has placed a wall of protection around you, but accessing pornography causes a hole to form in your protective membrane, and demons of lust and perversion gain entrance into your life.

He who digs a pit will fall into it, and whoever breaks through a wall will be bitten by a serpent.

Ecclesiastes 10:8 NKJV

Viewing pornography invites the most evil, nasty, unsafe and abusive creatures right into your heart and mind, into your most private place. Demons are dirty vermin who have no consideration for you or your loved ones. These unclean spirits behave like the imaginary creatures called vampires, only these demons are not imagined; they are real, and they want to take up residence inside of you. They cannot be bargained with, cannot be stopped, and they will never leave you. Even when you die, they will pass into a close relative as part of your inheritance. One viewing of porn will give you a lifelong companion who will be putting intrusive thoughts into your mind and causing unwanted feelings to well up inside of you, driving you towards more and more sexual sin and abuse. If you are a parent, a church leader, or in any position of authority, the demons will also be able to attack those who are under your spiritual care.

Pornography is powerfully addictive, and the seductive, intense cravings you experience come from demons. With these demons inside you, it is almost impossible to stop doing it. Demons will flash seductive images into your mind, stirring up feelings of lust and perversion, driving you to do things that leave you feeling dirty and degraded.

They cannot be bargained with, cannot be stopped, and they will never leave you.

The devil uses pornography to lead you further and further into sexual sin, and if you let him, he will take you on a journey into same-sex attraction and every form of immorality. Pornography is one of the ways by which the blight of homosexuality and pedophilia is exploding in our lands.

> ***Flee sexual immorality. Every sin that a man does is outside the body, but he who commits sexual immorality sins against his own body.***
>
> **1 Corinthians 6:18 NKJV**

Your only hope is the Lord Jesus Christ. Only Jesus can forgive you of your sins, and only in the name of Jesus can you drive out demons.

Jesus desires to set you free and clean you up. He will come to your aid, set you free, and give you a brand-new start in life if you let Him. Bring your sin to the Lord and ask Him to help you, and then make a decision to stop doing it, which is called repentance. When you repent and cast the demons out, you will immediately start to feel better, and resisting the temptation to sin becomes so much easier. See Chapter 14 to learn more about how to be delivered from demons.

> ***Your only hope is the Lord Jesus Christ.***

An interesting account of these spiritual principles in action is found in 2 Chronicles 14 and 15. King Asa came to power when the land was infested with sin, similar to our nation today. People were viewing sexually unclean images, demons were afflicting the people, and the land was unsafe to live in. King Asa removed the pornographic images and idols, dethroned those who served the devil, and cleansed the land of sin. He then ordered the people to serve the Lord and obey His commands, and he rebuilt the walls of the towns and cities. When the enemy came, the people had safe places to shelter in, and they were wholly with the Lord and able to access God's power to rout the enemy.

This account demonstrates the principles of spiritual warfare in action and how to defeat the enemy when he comes against you.

- Identify and deal with the sin in your life.
- Make a decision to stop doing it.
- Ask God to forgive you.
- Remove porn and sinful practices from your life.
- In Jesus' name, command all demons to leave you.
- The spiritual walls of protection will subsequently be rebuilt in your life.
- When the enemy comes against you, you will be able to defeat him.
- You become the victor, not the victim.
- You will live in peace and victory over all the works of the devil.

Turn away from sin. Stop doing it and ask the Lord to cleanse your life and rebuild the protective walls around you. Study Psalm 91 because it reveals how the Lord wants to lead us into victory over all the power of the devil.

> ***We live within the shadow of the Almighty, sheltered by the God who is above all gods. This I declare, that he alone is my refuge, my place of safety; he is my God, and I am trusting him. For he rescues you from every trap and protects you from the fatal plague. He will shield you with his wings! They will shelter you. His faithful promises are your armor. Now you don't need to be afraid of the dark anymore, nor fear the dangers of the day; nor dread the***

plagues of darkness, nor disasters in the morning.

Psalm 91:1-6 TLB

HOW TO LIVE A PORN FREE LIFE

Wherever possible, you need to remove any source of explicit or seductive images from your life. It is difficult to avoid billboards and people walking down the street dressed in a highly sexualized manner, but you must be careful what you choose to set your eyes on. Be wary when watching TV, movies, the internet, Facebook, TikTok, YouTube, music videos, and live performances of so-called entertainers. Nightclubs and bars where people dress provocatively and misbehave are unsuitable for those who want to live godly lives. Jezebel spirits are at work throughout society, encouraging immorality and indecency, promoting overtly sexualized dressing, and displaying fornication and homosexuality in movies, TV, and advertising, as normal human behavior. There is nothing wrong with a woman dressing in fine clothing that enhance her form, with beautiful hair styling, makeup, and jewelry. However, dressing in sexually aggressive attire like a prostitute is entirely different. Harlots dress to seduce people into having sex with them.

If you are not a hooker, don't dress like one.

There has never been a time like this when Jezebel spirits have gained widespread influence worldwide. The very airways are polluted as millions of indecent images silently fly through the air all around us. Almost every person has a cell phone that is capable of receiving explicit, hard-core pornography within a matter of seconds. Even young children have access to cell phones. The internet has made pornography one of Satan's most potent weapons. Porn is not even considered indecent anymore. Indecent images now refer to things like pedophilia. When, where, and how did pornography cease from being called indecent? The porn industry is totally demonic and highly addictive.

CASE STUDY ONE

I counseled a man whose teenage son had told him he was homosexual. His son said that he wanted to begin visiting places where homosexuals congregated so that he could start having physical relations with other men. His parents were alarmed because their son was still young and because they had no idea that he had these desires. During the next few days, the boy shared with them that he had been accessing pornography on the internet and had become addicted to it and that it had taken over his life. He watched some homosexual acts and started fantasizing about them. When he continued to access homosexual porn, the thought came to him that maybe he was a homosexual himself. Time passed, and eventually, he couldn't stop himself from telling his parents about his urge to begin meeting men and having sex with them. His parents were both Christians who loved their son and wanted to keep him safe from the homosexual scene, but they didn't want to suppress his sexuality either. They decided to introduce him to a man they knew in another church who was a practicing homosexual but who also called himself a Christian so that this man could educate him about how to live as a homosexual and stay safe when beginning a relationship. The father told me about the situation and how difficult it was for them. He said that they felt they needed to encourage their son into a homosexual lifestyle but also protect him from getting involved with random strangers and men much older than himself. We had a brief discussion about the stance they had taken, and I said that what they were doing was unscriptural and wrong. The man disagreed with me, saying that he needed to guide his son well and that homosexuality was not something to be concerned about.

OBSERVATIONS

The boy was allowed to access the internet without supervision and, from a young age, had been accessing pornography. Demons had come into him, leading him into more and more deprived content until he began to look at homosexual porn. Demons of homosexuality then began to fill his mind with lust for men. After some time, the boy decided that because he was having such intense lustful thoughts, he must be a homosexual. There was no teaching at church about such things, and the school he attended spoke very highly of people who were homosexual, saying that it was something commendable that needed to be celebrated. Eventually, he decided to experience sex with other men and told his parents about his intentions. His parents had made a series of errors with their son. They had decided to join a church because it was involved in social action and had an active children's ministry. However, the church was spiritually weak and refused to preach about homosexuality because they had a respectable place in the community and didn't want to upset anyone. A lack of spiritual covering over the family allowed the devil to attack their son. The parents should have realized the need to monitor their child's internet use, including what he did when visiting his friends' houses. When the teenager announced his intentions, they should have found a new church and sought advice from a godly Pastor. Taking a vulnerable young person to a homosexual man to be educated in how to have same-sex relations was a tragic error of judgment.

After our meeting, I reflected on the parents' choices and how they had arrived at such a disastrous place in life.

SOLUTION

The Christian walk is simple, although only sometimes easy to do. Join a church with a godly minister who isn't afraid to preach the Word of God. Live according to the Bible and protect your family physically and spiritually. If sin occurs, know that God loves you and bring the matter to Him. Stop doing it and take authority over all demons that came into your life and kick them out. Make changes to your life to protect you and your family from temptation and sin. If the internet causes someone under your care to sin, throw it away. Get rid of computers and cell phones. Carefully monitor who your children spend time with, and only allow them to visit houses that have the same spiritual standards as yourself. Move your children away from state schools that encourage homosexuality because this is a form of child abuse. Home educate your children or send them to a school that holds traditional values.

> ***Sin begins with a single thought.***

> ***And if your right hand causes you to sin, cut it off and throw it away. For it is profitable for you that one of your members should perish, and not that your whole body be thrown into hell.***

Matthew 5:30

SEXUAL FANTASY

Sin begins with a single thought.

Be in control of your thoughts at all times. You are not powerless over what thoughts run through your mind. Sexual fantasy is the companion of pornography. The problem with masturbation is sexual fantasy. Fantasizing about having sex with someone in your mind is not harmless. It is a sin, and it will begin to link you to the person in an unhealthy way.

> ***"You have heard that it was said by the ancients, 'You shall not commit adultery.' But I say to you that whoever looks on a woman to lust after her has committed adultery with her already in his heart.***
>
> **Matthew 5:27-28**

Sin gives the devil a place in your life.

> ***Be angry but do not sin. Do not let the sun go down on your anger. Do not give place to the devil.***
>
> **Ephesians 4:26-27**

Allowing sinful thoughts to play out in your mind will give place to the devil in your life.

You must rid yourselves of all sexual fantasies and command any demons that entered you through those thoughts to leave immediately.

> ***Sin gives the devil a place in your life.***

The mind is the interface between the physical and spiritual worlds. The devil can throw thoughts into our minds; we must always be on guard. We are NOT powerless over thoughts that come to us. We can dismiss wrong thinking and refuse to allow ungodly thoughts to stay. We are the doorkeepers of our minds, and we must be alert and diligent to whatever we find ourselves thinking about.

For though we walk in the flesh, we do not war according to the flesh. For the weapons of our warfare are not carnal, but mighty through God to the pulling down of strongholds, casting down imaginations and every high thing that exalts itself against the knowledge of God, bringing every thought into captivity to the obedience of Christ.

2 Corinthians 10:3-5

A person can be tempted to fantasize about having sex with another person.

We are NOT powerless over thoughts that come to us. We can dismiss wrong thinking and refuse to allow ungodly thoughts to stay.

Demons cannot read our thoughts, but they sense what people are thinking about, and they will begin to throw ideas into your mind and start to direct your fantasy. If a person is watching pornography or watching sexualized singers or entertainers, demons of lust will attack you, and sexual thoughts will flood into your mind. Images you look at become imprinted on your brain, and you will find yourself fantasizing about them and becoming drawn toward sinful sexual activity. Demons will lead you on a fantasizing journey, starting with normal sex and gradually becoming more depraved. Adultery, homosexuality, multiple partners, group sex, and sex with strangers will begin to occupy your fantasies. Demons will lead you into perversions such as anal sex, homosexuality, and then to pedophilia. Satan is aggressively sexualizing society through TV, the movie industry, entertainers, and pornography.

Sexual fantasy is so dangerous. Satan will use it to lead you into sexual sin. Many people are led by demons into adultery, homosexuality, and pedophilia because they don't exert self-control over their thought lives.

We are commanded to TAKE OUR THOUGHTS CAPTIVE! and control what we allow to occupy our minds. If a thought is negative, tell it to leave in Jesus' name, and then FORCE YOURSELF TO THINK OF GOOD AND WHOLESOME THINGS!

Open your Bible and begin to read the Word of God over yourself. Reading out loud is so powerful. Put a worship song on and start praising the Lord. People passively allow demons to give them fantasies, which gradually become more and more depraved. This is a well-worn demonic pathway into homosexuality. Demons will lead you into evil sexual practices such as homosexuality, bestiality, sadomasochism, and pedophilia. Pornography becomes imprinted on your mind, and you will continue to access it through the stored images long after you have ceased looking at the pictures. These images need to be broken in the name of Jesus, and the mind re-trained to focus on good things instead. The mind is like a muscle. You can train it and become able to control your thought life. Satan has easy access to your life if you have a weak mind.

The more you control your thoughts, the stronger your mind will become.

Repent from keeping stored images or fantasies in your mind and tell the demons associated with them to leave you in Jesus name, then ask the Holy Spirit to dismantle and burn up these images. Do not even fantasize about your spouse. Focus on them as they are, and be careful to avoid fantasy when making love with them, especially if those fantasies involve other people.

Sin begins with a single thought.

The devil uses various things to weaken our minds and make us increasingly passive. For example, things such as cannabis, too much alcohol, repetitive music, yoga, eastern meditation, chanting, blanking the mind, and endless hours of TV, amongst other things. Depression, discouragement, low self-worth, and impure thoughts will take root in your mind if you let them, as will fear and anxiety. Take authority over such thoughts and throw them out of your mind. It will be difficult at first because the devil will tell you that you need to explore and accommodate such thoughts into your life, but the scripture says that you need to cast them down and be self-controlled.

The more you control your thoughts, the stronger your mind will become.

> ***Submit yourselves therefore to God. Resist the devil, and he will flee from you.***

James 4:7 KJV

> ***For God has not given us the spirit of fear; but of power, and of love, and of a sound mind.***

2 Timothy 1:7

I know of an example of a Christian minister whose life was ruined via demonic fantasizing. He allowed demons to lead him into sexual sin. Demons will always try to lead people into homosexuality and pedophilia.

CASE STUDY TWO

I knew of a Christian minister who lived alone without a wife. He used to relieve himself sexually by fantasizing in his mind and masturbating. He didn't think he was doing anything wrong because he wasn't physically involved with anyone. He formed the image of an imaginary woman in his mind, and he would visit her several times a week and fantasize about having sex with her while masturbating. Over time, the image of the woman began to change. She became younger and younger until one day she was just 16 years old. The man knew he needed to control his fantasizing and not begin seeing her younger than this, but he couldn't help himself and began imagining her as a child. He continued to visit her in his mind until she was just eight years old. The girl was fictitious and did not resemble anyone he had ever seen, so he justified his fantasizing and continued doing it. He felt guilty about what he was doing but continued anyway and hid the dark secret in his mind. One day, there was a knock on the door of the vicarage. He opened the door, and there was a woman with a young girl. The woman explained to him that she was new in town and was going to a job interview but had been let down by her babysitter. She asked if the minister could look after her daughter for an hour until she returned. The man agreed, but when he looked at the girl, he was shocked to see that it was the child he had been fantasizing about, even though he had never physically seen her before. He brought her into the house and couldn't stop himself from sexually molesting her. The girl told her mother, who called the police, and the man was arrested. He confessed to the crime and was sentenced to prison.

OBSERVATIONS

This account is a classic case study of how the devil will lead you into sin if you are unaware of his schemes. The mind is the interface between the spirit world and the physical world. Demons can throw thoughts into your mind from outside of you, and we need to examine what we are thinking about and discard anything that is contrary to God's ways. When the man began to masturbate and fantasize, demons of sexual lust and immorality were empowered in his life, and they started to throw thoughts and images into his mind. The demons began to direct his fantasies and lead him into more and more depraved imaginary behaviors. It is easy for demons to arrange for us to sin if we willfully disobey God's commandments. The demons put the image of the woman into his mind, then began to make alterations to her, gradually making her younger and younger, until the day came when they succeeded in getting him to imagine her as a young girl. The devil makes plans for you to follow, and his demons put the image of the young girl into the man's head and then arranged for him to have physical access to her. The minister sinned, and lives were destroyed. The man lost the battle by allowing ungodly thoughts and images into his mind. He could have told the devil to get away from him and take his disgusting thoughts with him, but he was ignorant of spiritual warfare and fell victim to a simple attack from the enemy. What are we teaching ministers in seminary? Indeed, Hosea 4:6 and Isaiah 5:13 are relevant today.

Every sin begins with a single thought that goes unchecked.

> ***My people are destroyed for lack of knowledge.***
>
> **Hosea 4:6 KJV**

Therefore my people are gone into captivity because they have no knowledge.

Isaiah 5:13 KJV

Imagination is a wonderful thing in itself, but it needs to be monitored and used in a godly way, otherwise the enemy will use it against us for his own purposes. This minister's pathway into sin began with a single thought that he failed to take captive and discard. Secular therapists will tell you that anything is permitted in your mind as long as you don't act it out in real life. This concept is the teaching of demons.

It is better to suffer the inconvenience of having no access to the internet if it means living a victorious Christian life.

Every sin begins with a single thought that goes unchecked. The minister in the case study who fell into sin was mistaken in thinking he wasn't hurting anyone by imagining himself having sex with people in his mind. Jesus was clear that if we fantasize about sex with someone, it is just as serious as if we had physical sex with them. Committing sexual sin will always empower demons in your life, and their influence over you grows as you indulge in imaginary sex. We go where we are looking, and once we begin to imagine sinning sexually, it will only be a matter of time before we do so physically.

"You have heard that it was said by the ancients, 'You shall not commit adultery.' But I say to you that whoever looks on a woman to lust after her has committed adultery with her already in his heart. And if your right eye causes you to sin, pluck it out and throw it

away. For it is profitable that one of your members should perish, and not that your whole body be thrown into hell.

Matthew 5:27-29

Jesus explained that if you look at someone and imagine having sex with them, you are guilty of immorality. He says that if your eye causes you to sin, pluck it out and throw it away. This means we are to carefully guard what we are looking at with our eyes and imagination. Pornography is an example of a pathway into sin that we must pluck out of our lives and throw away. Maybe you need to get rid of your cell phone, laptop, or TV. Life continues without these things.

Take authority over your thoughts and make your mind your servant, not your master.

It is better to suffer the inconvenience of having no access to the internet if it means living a victorious Christian life.

The story of Samson in Judges 14, which I previously referred to, is a classic example of how someone foolishly strays into the vicinity of sin. Samson knew that eating grapes was forbidden, but he still walked past the vineyards to look at the grapes. Do not become intrigued by porn or think that you are strong enough to look at provocative images. It is like standing too close to a cliff edge. Stay two steps away from it at all times. So it is with sin. Stay two steps away from it, lest you fall and hurt yourself.

denying ungodliness and worldly lusts, we should live soberly, righteously, and godly, in this present world.

Titus 2:12 KJV

Take authority over your thoughts and make your mind your servant, not your master.

For though we walk in the flesh, we do not war according to the flesh. For the weapons of our warfare are not carnal, but mighty through God to the pulling down of strongholds, casting down imaginations and every high thing that exalts itself against the knowledge of God, bringing every thought into captivity to the obedience of Christ,

2 Corinthians 10:3-5 NKJV

Satan has made such inroads into contemporary thinking that we think we should indulge every thought and feeling we have, even if it is contrary to God's Word. We are commanded to carefully examine every thought and imagination to see if it is in obedience to Christ and then cast down everything that is opposed to God's ways.

I know of many marriages, even Christian marriages, that have been destroyed because one of them began to have feelings of homosexuality. The advice they usually receive is that they need to indulge their feelings and not deny or suppress their desires but see where they lead them. This passive response to demonic attack always ends in disaster. I have seen people leave marriages and begin homosexual relationships, thinking that it is simply inevitable. You are not powerless over your thoughts and feelings! Do not indulge yourself with ungodly imaginations.

Refuse all reasonings, feelings, or ideas that come to you if they contradict the scriptures.

Speak the name of Jesus and tell them to leave! Lust and perversion will come to you as thoughts and feelings, and they will take control of you if you allow them to.

> ***Let the words of my mouth, and the meditation of my heart, be acceptable in thy sight, O Lord.***
>
> **Psalm 19:14 KJV**

It's just a thought or a feeling. You don't have to listen to it or let it control you in any way. Your mind belongs to you, so it is up to you to decide what happens in your thought life. You can't always stop thoughts from flitting across your mind, but you can choose to disregard them if they don't fit in with what you want to be thinking about. Another way of saying it is that you can't stop a bird from flying over your head, but you can stop it from landing on you and building a nest in your hair.

Refuse all reasonings, feelings, or ideas that come to you if they contradict the scriptures.

You are NOT powerless over thoughts or feelings. Stop being a passive victim and regain control of your mind.

> ***He who has no rule over his own spirit is like a city that is broken down and without walls.***
>
> **Proverbs 25:28**

Rise up and deal with unwanted thoughts, imaginations, and feelings. Use your authority in the name of Jesus and tell them to leave you and never return, then force yourself to focus on what God is saying to you through His Word.

> ***Submit yourselves therefore to God. Resist the devil, and he will flee from you.***

James 4:7 KJV

Do not be passive. Resist the devil and his activity in your life. Speak out loud and declare scripture over yourself until you regain control of your mind. Put a Godly sermon on, or listen to some worship music to help you focus your mind on things that are wholesome and positive.

> ***Finally, brothers, whatever things are true, whatever things are honest, whatever things are just, whatever things are pure, whatever things are lovely, whatever things are of good report, if there is any virtue, and if there is any praise, think on these things.***

Philippians 4:8

> ***Lust desires to get, at the expense of others, while love desires to give, at the cost of self.***

2 Samuel 11 is an example of how unchecked thoughts can lead to sin and devastation. King David had thoughts about staying at home instead of going to war. He then had a thought about Bathsheba that he should have

dismissed, and then he thought about committing murder, and the story goes downhill from then on.

Sexual fantasy gives place to the devil and will lead you into many sins, including homosexuality. Fantasy gives birth to lust, which is always selfish and unloving. Sex in a loving marriage between a husband and wife is satisfying and fulfilling, where the couple gives to each other. Sex outside of the Lord's design order is unfulfilling and self-serving.

Lust desires to get, at the expense of others, while love desires to give, at the cost of self.

Sex outside God's order may be exotic and ecstatic, but it will never be satisfying and ends in loneliness and unfulfillment. Sexual sin does not just occur physically; it happens in your mind as well.

> ***You will keep him in perfect peace, whose mind is stayed on You, because he trusts in You.***

Isaiah 26:3

For further reading about managing intrusive thoughts I recommend a book called "Your Thoughts Are Killing You" by Marybeth Wuenschel.

Chapter Eight

TEMPTATION

YOU GO WHERE YOU'RE LOOKING

Satan is an angelic being who used to be called Lucifer. He was created to serve before the throne of Almighty God. He fell into the sin of Pride when he was tempted to receive worship for himself. He also tempted other angels to follow him and rebel against God; consequently, he and all who had joined him were decommissioned and thrown out of heaven. Lucifer, who was then renamed Satan, became known as the tempter.

He tempted the angels in heaven.

He tempted Eve in the garden.

He tempted Cain to murder his brother.

He tempted Israel to worship other gods.

He tempted King David with Bathsheba.

He tempted Judas with money.

He tempted Ananias and Sapphira to lie.

He will tempt you.

Satan is so deluded with Pride that he even thought he could tempt Almighty God.

> ***Jesus said to him, "It is written again, 'You shall not tempt the Lord your God.'" Again, the devil took him to a very high mountain and showed him all the kingdoms of the world and their splendor. "All this I will give you," he said, "if you will bow down and worship me." Then Jesus said to him, "Get away from here, Satan! For it is written, 'You shall worship the Lord your God, and Him only shall you serve.'"***

Matthew 4:7-10

The devil assumed that Jesus would desire glory and power for Himself, but Jesus came to serve, not to be served, and His only thought was to honor His Father in heaven.

HOW TO OVERCOME TEMPTATION

Jesus resisted temptation because there were no evil desires in His heart for temptation to attach itself to. Here lies the key to gaining victory over temptation. Deal with the ungodly desires you have allowed to flourish in your heart. Worldliness is the great enemy of the Christian.

> ***if your aim is to enjoy the evil pleasure of the unsaved world, you cannot also be a friend of God.***

James 4:4 TLB

When we love what the world offers, we are a sitting duck to the devil's temptations.

Temptation is greatly empowered when we have desires for forbidden things in our hearts. If we keep company with the world's culture and allow our minds to be filled with ungodly thoughts and images, we will have the wrong desires growing inside of us.

> ***Love not the world, neither the things that are in the world. If any man love the world, the love of the Father is not in him. For all that is in the world, the lust of the flesh, and the lust of the eyes, and the pride of life, is not of the Father, but is of the world.***
>
> **1 John 2:15-16 KJV**

Allowing unrighteous thoughts and images into your mind will lead to wrong desires growing inside of you. The person who falls into sexual sin will have already allowed the desire for this sin to be in their heart.

When we love what the world offers, we are a sitting duck to the devil's temptations.

CASE STUDY ONE

There was a Christian minister who preached about sexual purity but who was set up by people who wanted to destroy his ministry. One night, they put a prostitute naked on the bed in his hotel room. He came into the room, saw her, and committed adultery. The people had hidden cameras in the room, and his life was destroyed. How could this happen? Sadly, this kind of thing happens to so many gospel ministers. It was because he already had these desires hidden in his heart. That which you minister to will attack you. The man had been ministering to people who were struggling with sexual immorality, and the devil counter-attacked with the very thoughts and feelings he was preaching against. The man should have been aware of Satan's operating principles and been on guard against demons of lust and sexual immorality. God has plans for your life, but Satan also has plans for you. Typically, a minister like this could face a busy schedule, tiredness, and too much time away from his family. Maybe he had been browsing the internet in his hotel room instead of reading his Bible and praying as he usually did. Somehow, he had lowered his guard and allowed impure thoughts to run across his mind unchecked, which awakened ungodly desires within him, resulting in his failure to resist temptation when it came along. The minister should have been focusing on the Lord and His Word; then, when temptation came along, he would have fled just like Joseph did when Potiphar's wife offered herself to him (Genesis 39:7-12).

So many men of God fall in similar circumstances. You must be so careful in ministry. A person can be on fire in the pulpit and yet fall into sin a few hours later.

There are times when we become more vulnerable to temptation. Be aware of the things that make you more susceptible to sinful desires and put strategies in place to keep yourself safe.

People can struggle at times with things such as complacency, tiredness, boredom, loneliness, laziness, receiving ungodly advice, discouragement, low mood, hormonal issues, marital problems, or feeling that nothing is really happening in their lives. Some people struggle when they are on their own, and others become overloaded when they are constantly around other people. You need to know yourself and your limitations to stay safe and focused in life. We need to work hard, but God understands that we also need to take sufficient rest to be regenerated, which is why He gave us the Sabbath to take a break once a week. We also need other times of rest, recuperation, and recovery to keep ourselves balanced and refreshed. For some people, this can be sitting quietly on their own reading a book; for others, it can mean spending lots of time meeting new people and doing things with their friends and family. We are all different and become rejuvenated in different ways.

> ***In the spring of the year, the time when the kings go out to battle, David sent out Joab and his officers, all of Israel with him. They brought to ruin the Ammonites and besieged Rabbah, but David remained in Jerusalem. One evening when David arose from his bed and was walking on the roof of the king's house, from the roof he saw a woman bathing; and the woman was very beautiful.***

2 Samuel 11:1-2

King David had done so well in serving the Lord and leading his people in a godly manner, but maybe he'd become weary and complacent, which led to his decision to stay at home instead of going to war. It then looks like David had been sleeping during the day, maybe after a lengthy lunch with too much wine. He wakes up in the evening unfocused, with nothing to do, and walks out onto the terrace, where he sees Bathsheba bathing in her garden.

The greatest spiritual battle we will ever face is to maintain our daily time with the Lord, praying and reading the Bible.

This is a classic case of Satan putting a plan together to entice someone into committing adultery. The devil had started by putting ideas into his head about needing a break from fighting, which David should have checked out with the Lord. He didn't do this and stayed home when his army went out to fight. With nothing to do and no focus in life, the king was now vulnerable to Satan's plans for adultery to take place. When he should have been fighting the enemy side by side with his friend Uriah, he ended up lying side by side with Uriah's wife, Bathsheba. King David was in the wrong place at the wrong time and consequently fell into sexual sin.

Satan will patiently prepare you for his temptations, manipulating circumstances and setting traps for you to fall into. We need to know ourselves, our needs and weaknesses, and we must listen to God's leadings and promptings and give no place to the devil in our lives.

The greatest spiritual battle we will ever face is to maintain our daily time with the Lord, praying and reading the Bible.

We need to listen to the Holy Spirit's guidance, not go on holiday when we should be at war, and not fighting the enemy when we should be resting.

Our response to a thought so often determines the outcome.

Bathsheba could have also been set up by the devil. Perhaps she was feeling lonely and neglected by her husband? Maybe she knew that the king was alone in his palace and would take a walk on the terrace in the evening? It is possible that the devil was at work in both their lives, plotting their downfall.

CASE STUDY TWO

I heard of a minister who found himself alone in a foreign city. He was happily married and had never fallen into sexual sin. One evening after ministering, he decided to go for a walk to see what the city was like. He was walking past a sex club, which he had no experience of, when he suddenly decided to go in and have a quick look to see what it was all about. He went in and saw a woman dancing on the stage. He left immediately, but the image of the naked woman was imprinted on his mind, and for the first time in his life he became consumed with lust and impure thoughts. The minister fell into sexual sin, and it was ten years before he could finally break free and be delivered from this lifestyle. For this man, the problem was curiosity and being in the wrong place at the wrong time. Why was he ministering away from home without his wife or a ministry companion? Why did he go for a walk past sex clubs late at night? Had he been thinking about what happens in these places? The devil will set you up if you are not on guard and determined to be in the right place, at the right time, and doing the right things with the right people. Take every thought and feeling captive to the obedience of Christ.

Refusing to allow sinful desires to exist in your heart will enable you to resist temptation.

Our response to a thought so often determines the outcome.

We go where we are looking. As much as possible, do not allow yourself to be in a situation where you could be tempted. Guard your eyes, ears, and mind, and be aware that the devil can put a plan together, manipulating circumstances to entice you into sin. When the man walked past the sex club, demons of immorality saw him, and in order to draw him in, they threw thoughts of curiosity into his mind, making him feel intrigued about what happened inside such a place. When he entered the club "just to have a quick look," he gave permission to these demons to come into his life. He left the club, but these unclean spirits went home with him and began to afflict him with feelings of lust and immorality. He suffered from "sex addiction" for the next ten years before finally receiving the ministry and deliverance he needed.

> ***fill your minds with those things that are good and that deserve praise: things that are true, noble, right, pure, lovely, and honorable.***

Philippians 4:8 GNT

We become susceptible to sin when we harbor evil desires in our hearts. To overcome temptation, we need to have our minds renewed so that we live in fellowship with the Holy Spirit at all times.

> ***When all kinds of trials and temptations crowd into your lives my brothers, don't resent them as intruders, but welcome them as friends! Realize that they come to test your faith and to produce in you the quality of endurance.***

James 1:2-3 (PHILLIPS)

James 1:2-3 says we need to welcome temptations and trials because they expose what is in our hearts. Our flesh rises to the surface so that it can be dealt with. God does not want us to clean ourselves up before coming to Him. He wants us to be honest with Him and talk to Him about our failures, asking Him to deal with those wrong desires.

Refusing to allow sinful desires to exist in your heart will enable you to resist temptation.

Flies have little interest in clean surfaces, but one spot of filth will see them arriving from all directions. So it is when we allow sin to find a home within us. Demons will be attracted to your lust and the things that you covert, and they will tempt you to follow the longings of your heart. Do not tolerate unclean thoughts and desires. Deal with them at their source. You may need to stop listening to your favorite music or find some new friends. Find a church with a godly Pastor who is serving the Lord and get involved. Turn away from worldliness, meditate on the Word of God, and maintain a close walk with the Lord. The following verse is a crucial scripture when learning to refuse temptation.

> ***The pathway to sin begins when we allow a single ungodly thought or image to take up residence in our minds.***

> ***Present your bodies as a living sacrifice, holy, and acceptable to God, which is your reasonable service of worship. Do not be conformed to this world, but be transformed by the renewing of your mind, that you may prove what is the good and acceptable and perfect will of God.***

Romans 12:1-2

The pathway to sin begins when we allow a single ungodly thought or image to take up residence in our minds.

Our soul is the part of us that is tempted, not our spirit. Our soul is our mind and our will. It is our personality. The soul is like a sponge; it absorbs from the influences around it. Refrain from ungodly entertainment and media and be wary of keeping the wrong company.

> ***Blessed is the man who walks not in the counsel of the ungodly, nor stands in the path of sinners, nor sits in the seat of scoffers; but his delight is in the law of the Lord, and in His law he meditates day and night.***

Psalm 1:1-2

Watching TV and movies that portray homosexuality and promiscuity, together with music videos full of sexually explicit content, will negatively impact your heart's desires. Do not allow ungodly thoughts or images to sit in your mind. Look to God and His Word to strengthen and transform your mind. The promise in Romans 12:2 is that we will know the will of the Lord. We will become more aware of those things that please God and have a renewed knowledge of what is displeasing to Him. We will become more receptive to the Lord's voice and be enabled to discern Satan's whisperings. Our conscience will be renewed and strengthened by the Word of God to know right from wrong in situations we find ourselves in. In Genesis 39, Joseph did not fall into sin because he kept his eyes on the Lord—his physical eyes and his thought life. Therefore, because he had no desire in his heart to sin, when temptation came along, he was able to flee from it. If you find yourself tempted and falling into sin, it is because you are not meditating on the

Lord and His Word, the Bible. You are not delighting yourself in Him. Confess this failing to the Lord and ask Him to give you new desires in your heart, according to Psalm 37:4.

Delight yourself in the Lord, and He will give you the desires of your heart.

Delighting yourself is about falling in love with Jesus and wanting to spend time with Him. If you don't desire Him, you can ask Him to give you this desire and ask Him to provide you with more love for Him.

The Lord is speaking to you all the time, but you need to tune into His voice. Ask the Lord to re-sensitize you to hear Him, to renew your ability to sense His promptings. The Lord may be speaking to you about the TV show you are about to view, or the internet pages you browse. The movie you are watching may be harmless, but what about the commercials? We have been conditioned and dumbed down to passively accept the ungodly information and content coming at us. God will protect you from so much negativity around you if you listen to His voice and follow His leadings. It is not productive for Christians to go off into the world for their downtime and relaxation; we need to cultivate our relationship with the Lord and learn to be rejuvenated and restored by His Holy Spirit. There may be nothing wrong with watching a sporting event, but additional information from sponsors and advertisements will be flashing in your face that could be displeasing to the Lord. The demonic entertainment show at halftime will impact you more than you realize, creating a fertile environment for lust and rebellion to grow inside you, making you vulnerable to the devil's temptations. Be open and receptive to the still, quiet voice of the Lord, and follow his leadings.

The devil and the flesh will never tell you to study the Bible or pray in tongues. God will speak to us about positive activities such as prayer, Bible study, sharing the gospel, spending time with your family and friends, and working out. As you listen and obey the Lord, you will learn to recognize His voice more and more. Honestly examine your heart and ask the Lord to give you new desires that are pleasing to Him and command demons of lust and temptation to leave you, in Jesus' name.

Remember that our minds and hearts are like sponges, absorbing the influences around us, so it may be time to make some lifestyle changes.

Chapter Nine

JEZEBEL

THE DEMON WHO PRESIDES OVER HOMOSEXUALITY

> ***But I have a few things against you: You permit that woman Jezebel, who calls herself a prophetess, to teach and seduce My servants to commit sexual immorality.***

Revelation 2:20

Jezebel is the ruling spirit over homosexuality and all sexual sin. This spirit manifests through both men and women but is more commonly associated with women. I will refer to this demon as "her," as she often presents as female, or at least as something that is opposed to men's authority and headship. When I refer to Jezebel, I mean the demon whose personality is the same as the woman Jezebel in the Bible—a Jezebel spirit. Jezebel was the wife of King Ahab. She was a witch who opposed Godly order. We read about her in 1 Kings.

> ***But there was none like unto Ahab, which did sell himself to work wickedness in the sight of the Lord, whom Jezebel his wife stirred up.***

1 Kings 21:25 KJV

Ahab... took Jezebel... as his wife and went and served Baal and worshipped him. He raised an altar for Baal in the house of Baal, which he had built in Samaria. Ahab made an Asherah and did more to provoke the Lord God of Israel to anger than all the kings of Israel who preceded him.

1 Kings 16:31-33

Jezebel was the daughter of the pagan king Ethbaal, and she worshiped Baal. Jezebel led her husband to worship Baal and perform rituals before the Asherah poles. The demons that inspired her to rebel against God's way are still active in our society today. We refer to them as Jezebel spirits, and they have the same characteristics as the woman Jezebel in the Bible. Jezebels get alongside those in authority, influencing them to rebel against the Lord and His ways.

If there is ever any suggestion that the Bible is not our final authority on all matters, you can be sure that a Jezebel spirit is at work.

When Jezebel is in the house, the church stops speaking out against homosexuality and against sin in general. Social action groups replace prayer meetings. Teachings such as Spiritual Warfare and the Baptism in the Holy Spirit stop because someone (the Jezebel) feels they are divisive. Writings other than the scriptures are given equal place or begin to supersede the Bible. Climate crisis, inclusivity, and anti-discriminatory practice are preached. Churches take down the cross because people find it offensive, and pastors ask their members to educate themselves with unscriptural homosexual theology.

These are just some of the things that happen when the Jezebel spirit is present. This spirit operates like a snake. It slithers into homes and churches, into pulpits and ministries. Jezebel attaches itself to both men and women who are in Godly authority and will begin to exert influence over them. She makes men effeminate and women manly. Seeking to control others, she drains the life out of godly leaders and is an unseen force attempting to thwart the purposes of God.

Jezebels operate in ascending levels of power, using traits such as flattery and seduction, then manipulation, intimidation, and finally domination, as it seeks to control those in authority. She will typically target the husband, the pastor, the prophet, and the head of the church or the organization.

Jezebel will always attack the Word of God. She is opposed to the Bible, godly preaching, and prophecy.

If there is ever any suggestion that the Bible is not our final authority on all matters, you can be sure that a Jezebel spirit is at work.

A glaring example of Jezebel in action is seen in the Church of England. Jezebel has been tolerated in the church for many years and has coiled itself around the leadership, emasculating them and leading them astray. She has strategically replaced God-fearing men with her own servants and quietly promoted them into positions of authority within the church. While millions of people are dying and going to Hell, the Church of England is embroiled in endless debates about homosexuality.

Jezebel has cast a spell over the leadership, which has negated their authority and switched off their anointing. The church has become paralyzed by witchcraft and has forsaken its

God-given ministry. They can no longer take a moral stand against homosexuality. With Jezebel pulling the strings, this toothless church will campaign about homophobia, trans rights, socialism, and climate crisis while holding a deafening silence about healing the sick, casting out demons, raising the dead, and saving souls from an eternity in Hell. So much of the church today reminds me of what Jesus said of some religious leaders: they are like whitewashed tombs, clean on the outside, but on the inside they are full of dead men's bones.

This barrenness and confusion is the result of Jezebel in action, thwarting the purposes of God and leaving an empty façade of religion in place of a thriving church.

> ***"Woe to you, scribes and Pharisees, hypocrites! You are like whitewashed tombs, which indeed appear beautiful outwardly, but inside are full of dead men's bones and of all uncleanness."***

Matthew 23:27

We now have homosexual clergy and bishops, and Archbishops bless homosexual relationships. Same-sex marriage will soon be practiced throughout the church.

Jezebel emasculates godly leadership, usurping their authority and using it against them. This wicked spirit coils itself around the leaders, switching off their anointings and nullifying their ministries. She operates like a parasite, or a vampire, draining the spiritual authority and strength from godly ministers.

Jezebel is cunning and crafty. We feel the effects of this spirit, but it is often difficult to challenge and sometimes hard to know where or from whom it emanates. Her witchcraft will destroy the ministry without a God-fearing leader who refuses to be manipulated and controlled. Jezebel is a weaver of webs and craftiness. She is difficult to confront and remove once she has gained a position in a ministry or someone's life. The only way to deal with Jezebel is to be entirely intolerant of her.

Do not become embroiled in discussions or allow her to reason with you.

Jezebel sent a threatening message to Elija. He listened to it and was so intimidated that he ran from her and was defeated. Jezebel is too powerful for us to listen to her. Her words are laden with evil spiritual power, and we must be intolerant of her immediately we come across her. Otherwise, her words act like curses on us and begin to usurp our power and authority.

If anyone attempts to give credibility to anything contrary to scripture, you must oppose them wholly and immediately. Do not discuss it.

Jezebel loves to embroil God's people in interminable discussions and debates about the authority of scripture, climate crisis, homosexuality, and sin in general. Whenever there is an opposition to healing the sick, speaking in tongues, casting out demons, and prosperity, be sure that a Jezebel is in the house. The discussion about homosexuality must be about how we can lovingly rescue people from this sinful lifestyle and disciple them as Christians. It is a very short discussion that should last for one session of the church leadership and then be acted upon.

We should then focus our time on safeguarding issues such as how to keep our children safe from the infiltration of homosexuality in schools, the media, and society in general.

Jezebel will not stop until she is cast down and thrown out. Elijah failed to deal with Jezebel. He defeated her prophets and came against Baal worship but didn't deal with the source of the problem, the Jezebel in the land.

> ***And Ahab told Jezebel all that Elijah had done and how he had executed all the prophets with the sword. Then Jezebel sent a messenger to Elijah, saying, "So let the gods do to me and more also, if I do not make your life as the life of one of them by tomorrow about this time." When he saw that she was serious, he arose and ran for his life.***

1 Kings 19:1-3

Elijah killed the prophets of Baal and should have killed Jezebel, but he listened to her threat and allowed a witchcraft spirit of intimidation to come against him. We must stand up to the Jezebel coming against us. Elijah should have stood on God's word, the very word that he himself had prophesied about her death.

If anyone attempts to give credibility to anything contrary to scripture, you must oppose them wholly and immediately. Do not discuss it.

> ***And concerning Jezebel the Lord also spoke, saying, 'The dogs shall eat Jezebel by the wall of Jezreel.'***

1 Kings 21:23

Jezebel's witchcraft overpowered Elijah, and the Lord had to use King Jehu to execute judgment on her instead. King Jehu ordered Jezebel to be thrown down to her death, then trampled her underfoot.

> ***When Jehu came to Jezreel, Jezebel heard about it. She put black paint on her eyes, adorned her head, and looked down through the window. As Jehu entered in at the gate, she said, "Is everything all right, Zimri, murderer of his master?" And he lifted up his face toward the window and said, "Who is on my side? Who?" And two or three eunuchs looked down to him. He said, "Drop her down." So they dropped her down and some of her blood splattered on the wall and on the horses. Then he trampled her.***

2 Kings 9:30-33

This passage is interesting because it gives further insight into the workings of Jezebel. Jehu is coming to kill her and will not be intimidated. Jezebel then switches from making threats to seduction and manipulation. She painted her eyes as a seductress to persuade Jehu not to kill her. Everything Jezebel does is controlling. She will use intimidation, flattery, seduction, and threats to make you feel sorry for her, but the goal is always the same. She is trying to control you.

Confronting a Jezebel is often so difficult. Once the person knows you are on to them, they will usually evade an open meeting with you, choosing to ignore the call to accountability, and using an array of behaviors to deflect the focus away from them.

Churches that refuse to preach against homosexuality are under the intimidation of Jezebel, regardless of the excuses they make about not giving a clear lead on the matter.

Jezebel hides in plain sight.

Christian schools who employ homosexual teachers and tolerate 'rainbow' flags, because some children and parents want to give voice to homosexuality, are under the influence of Jezebel. Jezebel hides in plain sight. She is using the God-given symbol of the rainbow for her evil purposes. The rainbow is associated with judgment. God destroyed the world with a great flood because of sins such as homosexuality and other immoral activities. The Lord placed a rainbow in the sky as a sign that He would never send a worldwide flood again.

Incidentally, it is interesting to note that the so-called 'rainbow' colors used by sexual perverts contain only six colors, while God's rainbow contains seven colors. Jezebel's flag isn't a rainbow at all, it is simply a multi-colored symbol of rebellion. Sodom and Gomorrah were destroyed by fire because of the sin of homosexuality. Their destruction was a warning of the coming judgment on the world and eternal torment in the flames of Hell for all who live a lifestyle of sexual sin and who refuse to follow and serve the Lord Jesus Christ.

God condemned the cities of Sodom and Gomorrah to destruction by reducing them to ashes, making them an example to those afterward who would live ungodly lives.

2 Peter 2:6

The day of the Lord will come like a thief in the night, in which the heavens will pass away with a loud noise, and the elements will be destroyed with intense heat. The earth also and the works that are in it will be burned up.

2 Peter 3:10

And fear not them which kill the body but are not able to kill the soul: but rather fear him which is able to destroy both soul and body in Hell.

Matthew 10:28

Jezebel's flag isn't a rainbow at all, it is simply a multi-colored symbol of rebellion.

Men and women operating under a Jezebel spirit openly walk amongst us today. They must be challenged and confronted to prevent them from causing mischief, and also so that they have an opportunity to repent and follow a different path in life if they want to. When you confront a Jezebel, it will usually be the last time you see them. Jezebels are powerful people but will flee from those who refuse to be controlled by them. You must calmly and firmly challenge them and hold their manipulative behavior to account.

FURTHER WARNINGS ABOUT JEZEBEL

Married people must be careful about spending time alone with members of the opposite sex.

Do not be alone with someone who is not your spouse, to protect yourself from temptation, and also to be safe from false accusation.

Fellowship in the church must be holy and pure. Be wary of hugging people, and only do so when others are around. Do not travel alone with someone who isn't your husband or wife, and don't visit someone of the opposite sex unless their spouse is at home. Male leaders should not be hugging women who are not their wives, and vice versa. Christians are so gullible and fall easy prey to witches infiltrating their meetings.

Chapter Ten

RECOGNISING THE JEZABEL SPIRIT

WHO IS HIDING IN PLAIN SIGHT

Jezebel will always oppose the authority of the Bible.

This demon is the spiritual power behind homosexuality and immorality and will lead people into sexual sin. Jezebel loves to mock God. Transgenderism is a typical example of how she has misled people into rebelling against their God given identity and desecrating their bodies. Transgenders have a "trans agender", to manipulate and intimidate society into believing that a person can change their identity and re-identify. People are free to do what they want, but transgenderism is a mental illness, a state of believing that something which is false is true. We must not collude with people who claim such crazy things. We are being intimidated so much by this madness, and they are attempting to force us to say that their delusions are real.

> ***A woman must not wear man's clothing, nor is a man to put on a woman's clothing. For all that do so are abominations to the Lord your God.***

Deuteronomy 22:5

Transgenderism is a classic example of Jezebel.

Men who think they are women, and women who think they are men, with others who are neither. We are being pressured into using words such as trans, transgender, non-binary, and cisgender, instead of man and woman. Jezebel mocks and degrades those who are under her sway. Transgenderism is a mental illness. People who are confused and deluded about their identity need compassion and help, not collusion.

A man is an adult male and a woman is an adult female. Men have XY Chromosomes and women have XX Chromosomes.

> ***God created man in His own image; in the image of God He created him; male and female He created them.***
>
> **Genesis 1:27 KJV**

The presence of Jezebel can sometimes be seen by a person's language, demeanor, and the clothes they wear. Trousers can be worn by a woman and still be feminine, but if a woman deliberately wears clothes to look masculine, or if a man dresses to look feminine, we see Jezebel at work. Jewelry can also have spiritual significance. It is perfectly acceptable for a woman to wear a single earring in each ear, but having multiple piercings has an air of rebellion about it. It is occultic to have body piercings and tattoos, and a woman who wants to please the Lord should remove all excess piercings. Men should not have any earrings, piercings, or tattoos. When people come under the influence of Jezebel, piercings, tattoos, and unconventional clothing become desirable to the person, often accompanied by other rebellious behaviors. Women shave their heads, and men grow long hair. Hair styles and choice of colors give an indication of where a person is up to spiritually.

> ***Does even nature itself not teach you that if a man has long hair, it is a shame to him? But if a woman has long hair, it is a glory to her, for her hair is given her for a covering.***
>
> **1 Corinthians 11:14-15**

The demon of Jezebel is seen in music videos, advertising hoardings, media, and TV. People are seen wearing highly sexualized clothing, posing, and dancing provocatively. Women feel no shame in walking down the street dressed like prostitutes, because they've watched performances by pop stars and many others degrading themselves in such a way.

Men are often portrayed as effeminate, and homosexuality is presented as something normal and wholesome, and even trendy and desirable. Jezebel is manipulating men and women into rebellion against God, intimidating society, gaslighting, and canceling those who oppose her as she grows in prominence and visibility. Jezebel is manipulating, intimidating, dominating, coercing, and attempting to control society. Usurping the norm. Breeding rebellion. Mocking God. Perverting His order. Telling us that homosexuality is to be celebrated, that trans people are normal. Criminalizing any voice that disagrees with her. Brutalizing society.

Just like her master, Satan, Jezebel hates a face-to-face fight. She is a braggart and a bully, a person of boastful words and empty threats, who tries to win without exchanging blows. The giant called Goliath in 1 Samuel 17 was a typical example of how this evil operates. He looked enormous, with a big reputation and a boastful mouth. He spoke over God's people and intimidated them. Goliath used words to nullify and defeat the whole army of God. He didn't even have to raise a finger to strike terror and dread into the hearts of Gods people, he simply controlled them with words, rendering them powerless and defeated. David, however, looked to God and countered the words of Goliath with a greater truth. The battle was won even before physical contact was made. David chose to meditate on the Lord and His Word, rather than the empty threats of the enemy. Goliath trusted in his gods, while David relied on the Lord, which meant the battle became a contest between God and Satan. Goliath was defeated and had his head cut off. This is exactly how we deal with a Jezebel. We do not physically fight with them; it is a spiritual fight. We stand our ground and denounce their threats. We refuse to be intimidated by them.

> ***the Philistine cursed David by his gods. Then David said to the Philistine, "You come to me with a sword, a spear, and a shield, but I come to you in the name of the Lord of Hosts, the God of the armies of Israel, whom you have reviled. This day will the Lord deliver you into my hand. And I will strike you down and cut off your head.***

1 Samuel 17:43-46

Goliath was a powerful giant, a servant of the devil. David stood up to him and killed him by refusing to be intimidated by his words and his witchcraft power.

> ***Submit yourselves to God. Resist the devil, and he will flee from you.***

James 4:7

Goliaths' words were designed to drain the strength and faith out of David, because they were spiritual in nature. Words have the power of life and death, and in calling upon his gods, Goliath was tapping into spiritual power, or witchcraft.

> ***Death and life are in the power of the tongue.***

Proverbs 18:21 KJV

This giant was slain, but Satan has raised up a new champion he calls LBGTQIA+. The + is added because he is waiting to see if we are gullible enough to allow him to add more letters to the name. Maybe pedophilia will soon be added? Bestiality? Satan's agenda of homosexuality and transgenderism is an intimidating Goliath in our midst. Boasting, bullying, and threatening to impose itself on our families, our churches, and our country.

When a homosexual becomes established in a place, they begin to exert an influence over the environment, letting everyone know what they are, and demanding that their homosexuality is acknowledged, accepted, and also celebrated. Satan is a liar and a coward. He doesn't even have the courage to fight fairly. He goes for the young in our schools. He targets the weak and vulnerable in society. He casts spells and twists truth, changing the names of his perversions so that the homosexual is now "gay", and men and women who become confused about their identity are now "trans". The devil's wickedness is even traveling overseas to interfere with other countries. Where we once sent ministers of the gospel, we now send satanic emissaries, armed with the threat of withholding financial support if they don't adopt our sexual perversions and child sacrifice.

But this is what I have against you: you tolerate that woman Jezebel, who calls herself a messenger of God. By her teaching she misleads my servants into practicing sexual immorality.

Revelation 2:20 GNT

But I say that the things which the Gentiles sacrifice, they sacrifice to demons, and not to God. I do not want you to have fellowship with demons. You cannot drink the cup of the Lord and the cup of demons. You cannot be partakers of the Lord's table and of the table of demons. Do we provoke the Lord to jealousy? Are we stronger than He?

1 Corinthians 10:20-22

We see these same things in the Bible.

Obadiah went to meet Ahab and told him. And Ahab went to meet Elijah. When Ahab saw Elijah, Ahab said to him, "Are you he that troubles Israel?" And he answered, "I have not troubled Israel, but you and your father's house, in that you have forsaken the commandments of the Lord and you have followed the Baals. Now send word out and gather for me all Israel on Mount Carmel, along with the four hundred and fifty prophets of Baal and

the four hundred prophets of Asherah who eat at Jezebel's table."

1 Kings 18:16-19

Worshiping Baal involved homosexuality, prostitution, occult rituals, and child sacrifice. People stood before the sex symbol of Asherah and became inflamed with lust as demons attached themselves to them. This continues today as Jezebel entices people to stand before the spiritual Asherah poles of pornography.

Even the airways are polluted with demonic filth, as indecent images fly to cell phones and TV's. The people that watch such things become afflicted with demons of lust and perversion.

In modern times, one of the ways that Jezebel is worshipped is when people attend concerts to watch singers and dancers presenting highly sexualized, ungodly performances. The money, idolization, and devotion given to these performers is received as worship by the demon of Jezebel.

Truly, there is nothing new under the sun. Jezebel is active today, just as she was in Elijah's day, turning the hearts of the people against the Lord.

Jesus will never turn anyone away. No matter who you are, or what you have done, or what has been done to you. He loves you and wants you.

Jezebel and her witchcraft need to be exposed by the truth of the Lord Jesus Christ and His Word. Jesus is the opposite of Jezebel. She only uses people for her own purposes, but Jesus loves you unconditionally, even if you rebel against Him. Jesus is holy, pure, safe, non-controlling and life giving. He comes to set free all who are broken and bound by Jezebels abuses. Jesus offers forgiveness and a brand-new start in life. He will not force anyone to come to Him, but He eagerly waits for the moment when we choose to turn to Him.

Jesus will never turn anyone away. No matter who you are, or what you have done, or what has been done to you. He loves you and wants you.

> ***But God demonstrates His own love toward us, in that while we were yet sinners, Christ died for us.***

Romans 5:8

Baal and Asherah worship are the worship of demons and was explicitly forbidden by the Lord.

> ***Watch yourself so that you make no covenant with the inhabitants of the land where you are going, lest it become a snare in your midst. But you shall destroy their altars, break their sacred pillars, and cut down their Asherah poles for you shall not worship any other god, for the Lord, whose name is Jealous, is a jealous God, lest you make a covenant with the inhabitants of the land, and they prostitute themselves with their gods, and sacrifice to their gods, and someone invites you to eat of his sacrifice. And then you take of their daughters for your sons, and their daughters prostitute themselves after***

their gods. They will make your sons prostitute themselves after their gods.

Exodus 34:12-16

Christians should stand out in this world as people who live differently to those around them. The culture of the day should conform to the Bible and God's ways. The church does not need to become culturally relevant in society. Nobody will complain about our "church music" if they can come and be healed from every sickness and disease. We should be preaching salvation and repentance from sin and declaring God's extravagant love for all people, healing the sick and demonstrating forgiveness and love to those around us. People won't say we are out of touch if we drive their demons out and set them free from depression and mental illness. If a child is killed on the street, and we raise them back to life, who will say we are not culturally relevant?

What has been is the same as what will be, and what has been done is the same as what will be done; there is nothing new under the sun.

Ecclesiastes 1:9

There is indeed nothing new under the sun. Same old sins, same old demons. We even sacrifice our babies to Baal. Baal was the god of prosperity. How many people have murdered their child for the sake of financial benefit, or because having a baby was an inconvenience, not fitting in with their plans? Nowadays, a woman doesn't place her child into the oven of Molech, but she does open her legs

The church does not need to become culturally relevant in society.

and pay someone to murder her baby. Men are just as guilty of human sacrifice if they encourage or collude with the mother to kill their child. Abortion has become a socially acceptable way of murdering your own children. A woman can pay someone to kill her baby during her lunch break, then go back to work in the afternoon as though nothing has happened. We recoil in horror at the mention of Nazi death camps, then vote a servant of Satan into office, who encourages and supports this silent, sanitized holocaust of child sacrifice, that makes Hitlers final solution seem like a sick tea party. These evil politicians have overseen the murder of 1.5 BILLION children in the last 50 years. Baal and his side kick Jezebel have taught us to use words such as termination instead of murder, and fetus instead of baby. Baal and Jezebel use evil organizations such as Planned Parenthood to feed their insatiable bloodlust.

Maybe there is something more important than your finances to consider the next time you go to vote?

The demons who led people astray in biblical times are still around today. They are influencing culture just as they did thousands of years ago. Homosexuality, pornography, pedophilia, and sex with multiple partners are at pandemic levels throughout the land, along with unfaithfulness and abuse. Men want to identify as women, and woman as men, dishonoring the body given to them by the Lord. Self-harming by cutting the body is at epidemic levels, as demons gloat over the flow of human blood. We see cutting the body done by Baals prophets.

> ***They cried out loud and cut themselves with knives and spears according to***

their custom until the blood gushed out on them.

1 Kings 18:28

The spirits behind these behaviors are Jezebel and her despotic partner Baal.

But this is what I have against you: you tolerate that woman Jezebel, who calls herself a messenger of God. By her teaching she misleads my servants into practicing sexual immorality.

Revelation 2:20 GNT

Maybe there is something more important than your finances to consider the next time you go to vote?

The reason Jezebel wants people to commit sexual sin, and sin in general, is so that she can gain influence in their lives. Jezebel, just like her master Satan, hates human beings. There is a misguided belief that the devil is the one who wants you to enjoy a good sex life, whilst God is against it. Nothing could be further from the truth. God created us to enjoy sex, and gave us guidelines to keep us safe physically, emotionally, and spiritually. Jezebel does not care one bit about humans enjoying themselves. She only wants to rule us and cause as much pain and misery as possible, both in this life and for all eternity in Hell.

Jezebel is NOT the goddess of sexual pleasure. She is the goddess of sexual sin.

Jezebel operates like a parasite, attaching herself to people, persuading them to give her their authority, then using it against them, until they become mere puppets to do her bidding. Jezebel hates you and wants to break your heart.

> ***But there were false prophets, too, in those days, just as there will be false teachers among you. They will cleverly tell their lies about God, turning against even their Master who bought them; but theirs will be a swift and terrible end. Many will follow their evil teaching that there is nothing wrong with sexual sin. And because of them Christ and his way will be scoffed at.***

1 Peter 1:1-3 TLB

The Jezebel may be able to hide their true nature for a while, but over time their behavior will reveal their true identity.

> ***For such are false apostles and deceitful workers, disguising themselves as apostles of Christ. And no wonder! For even Satan disguises himself as an angel of light. Therefore it is no great thing if his ministers also disguise themselves as ministers of righteousness, whose end will be according to their works.***

2 Corinthians 11:13-14

Jezebels have both narcissistic and psychopathic traits. Jezebels operate in a spirit of witchcraft, which involves using spiritual power to manipulate and control others. Jezebels will use a whole bunch of tricks to gain a position in your life.

Jezebels will try to engage you in interminable debates about things such as homosexuality, the authenticity of scripture, the Baptism in the Holy Spirit, and spiritual warfare. Stand your ground and do not get drawn into such debates or discussions. You do not need to explain yourself to anyone. If someone disagrees with you about a foundational aspect of the faith simply show them what the Bible says, and if they disagree with the Bible, then close the discussion down. Do not reason with a Jezebel. You must not negotiate, discuss, argue, or debate with the Jezebel spirit, or those operating under the Jezebel spirit. It is a form of pride to do so, it is trusting in self rather than trusting in God, and pride comes before destruction.

Jezebel is NOT the goddess of sexual pleasure. She is the goddess of sexual sin.

We will inevitably come under counterattack from the Jezebel spirit. That which we minister to attacks us. People operating under a Jezebel spirit will have pride, self-righteousness, rebellion, and a refusal to come under godly authority. We must counter Jezebel as Jehu did. Cast her down without debate or engagement and trample on her. I do not mean we should physically harm anyone, because every person is precious to the Lord, I mean that we are to resist the spirit operating in them. Speak honestly and firmly to the person, letting them know that you do not tolerate their manipulative behavior. If needed, speak forthrightly to them, as Jesus did with Peter.

But Jesus turned and said to Peter, "Get behind Me, Satan! You are an offense to Me, for you are not mindful of the things that are of God, but those that are of men."

Matthew 16:23

Resolutely stand against Jezebels. Don't react to them or be drawn into discussions or arguments. Do not compromise in any way, nor be intimidated by them. Firmly resist them and be intolerant, trusting in the Lord completely.

You must not negotiate, discuss, argue, or debate with the Jezebel spirit, or those operating under the Jezebel spirit. It is a form of pride to do so,

Trust in the Lord with all your heart, And lean not on your own understanding; In all your ways acknowledge Him, And He shall direct your paths. Do not be wise in your own eyes; Fear the Lord and depart from evil. It will be health to your flesh, and strength to your bones.

Proverbs 3:5-8 NKJV

Chapter Eleven

JEZEBEL IN ACTION

CASE STUDIES

CASE STUDY ONE

A family joined a strong, Bible-believing church and immediately gave their support and encouragement to the minister. They brought finances and offered to use their giftings in church, which were readily accepted. One of the family became close friends with the minister and found that they shared a love of people and church work. Someone discerned that this new person in the church was, in fact, a homosexual with an agenda for the church. This was shared with the minister, but he dismissed these warnings and promoted the man to a leadership position in the youth ministry. This man then began to teach the youth that homosexuality was not wrong and that God is pleased with anyone who has same-sex feelings for others. People began to complain to the minister, but he failed to act. This man was then promoted onto the church leadership team and began to promote homosexuality as something excellent and wholesome. Several people called an emergency meeting of the whole church to express their alarm at this new teaching. In the meeting, the newly promoted leader spoke at length about the need to welcome homosexuals into the church because we need to be a place of love and acceptance of all people. The meeting lasted three hours, and several people spoke out against him. The leader, however, remained silent. At the end of the meeting, the man said that the cross needed to be removed from the church as well as the Bibles, because the people in the community would not enter the building if such things were on display. The minister closed the meeting and asked for unity and acceptance of one another. He said he wanted everyone to read and study two books, one supporting homosexual relationships between Christians and one that did not. He said everyone needed to make up their own mind on the subject.

At this time, several people left the church. After the meeting, the minister removed the cross from the church and supported the homosexual leader.

OBSERVATIONS

The minister himself was not walking with the Lord as he should have been and consequently became vulnerable to attack from the enemy. Anyone not in a close relationship with Jesus is not fit to lead God's people.

Jezebels will present themselves as helpful and valuable assets in a church or organization, often giving money and gifts to the leader. They will actively seek to gain a hold over the church's leader and his authority. When leaders fail to stand up to them, they grow stronger. The Jezebel will gradually unmask and denounce the things of God, constantly attacking God's Word. Jezebel takes legitimate authority off of people and uses it herself. In 2 Kings, we see Jezebel surrounded herself with eunuchs, men who had been emasculated.

The minister was being controlled by this Jezebel and found himself unable to stand up to him and keep the church safe. Many people were led astray and harmed because the minister yielded his authority to the Jezebel, and the church was destroyed.

CASE STUDY TWO

A church had an incident where a daughter of a family in church announced one day that she was homosexual. The church didn't want to upset anyone, so they had never preached about homosexuality. The family demanded that the girl be encouraged in church as a lesbian, but the leadership said that their biblical stance meant they couldn't do so. Soon afterward, the girl committed suicide, and the family publicly blamed the church. The minister announced that he had been at fault for not celebrating the woman's lesbianism, and he publicly repented from his former stance on homosexuality. The church has now become fully inclusive towards homosexuals, and they denounce the biblical texts regarding this sin. "Rainbow" colors, or rather multi-colored flags, decorate the church, and everyone is now welcome in their services, regardless of their beliefs or lifestyles.

OBSERVATIONS

The church had been under attack from Jezebel for some time. They ceased preaching against homosexuality because they didn't want to discourage people from attending the church. The minister was not in a close walk with the Lord and was not standing firmly on the Word of God. When an incident occurred where a woman committed suicide, he immediately acquiesced to the accusations leveled against him and became entirely dominated by the spirit of Jezebel. The woman who killed herself should have been told by the church that God loved her and wanted to heal her, but they refused to take a godly approach to address her needs. The minister was insecure in his relationship with God and the Bible, and he quickly yielded his spiritual authority to Jezebel under attack. Today that church has a fine set of buildings and is busy promoting sexual perversions and transgenderism. Community activities such as Yoga, coffee mornings, addiction groups, and slimming classes are available throughout the week. Christians take their children there to be encouraged to lead a homosexual lifestyle, and everyone is welcome, regardless of who you are or what you believe.

Everyone, that is, except the Lord Jesus Christ.

CASE STUDY THREE

A Bible-believing church appointed a new minister, a young man fresh out of seminary. The denomination appointed him because it had a shortage of ministers and promoted him prematurely, which was a mistake, as the man was not a mature believer and wasn't ready to lead God's people. The new minister held left-wing political views and began to impose those opinions on the church. He was outspoken on what he believed to be anti-discriminatory practice throughout society and the Bible. He was a feminist who seemed to dislike men in general. He supported women in the church who objected to patriarchal language, such as referring to God as Father. He preached that the Bible and the language used in the church were discriminatory against women. He organized the re-writing of the prayers and liturgy to make it less "sexist" and more "inclusive" towards women. One of the devil's most potent weapons is a sincere Christian who has been deceived, and this man unwittingly allowed a spirit of Jezebel into the church. God-fearing people became discouraged and started leaving, while those who felt that social justice issues were more important than preaching the gospel came to prominence in the church. People started having extramarital affairs, even in the leadership, and marriages began to fall apart. The minister preached about

God's love, but he was personally distant from his congregation and harsh towards those who needed encouragement and support. He gave his time to women with strong feminist views, encouraging them to change the church to suit their personal and political views. He became overly close to and inappropriate towards a married woman in church. Abortion began to be practiced to cover up sexual sin because unwanted pregnancy interfered with people's lives. A homosexual man began attending the church. He failed to receive the clear teaching, pastoral support, and deliverance that he needed. The minister encouraged him to marry a woman in church before he was ready to do so, and he then committed sexual offenses against her children. I later heard that he had committed suicide while in prison.

Everyone is welcome, regardless of who you are or what you believe. Everyone, that is, except the Lord Jesus Christ.

OBSERVATIONS

The head of the church, the family, or the organization is critical in giving a spiritual covering over everyone. This is why Jezebel will always strategically attack those in spiritual headship. She became the wife of King Ahab in 1 Kings so that she could influence and then rule the kingdom through Ahab.

In this unfortunate case, the Jezebel spirit entered the church when the minister arrived. There was a lack of spiritual discernment and wisdom in the elders in allowing such an unsuitable person to come in and lead God's people. The man yielded to the Jezebel spirit and replaced the authority of scripture with social action and the need to challenge everything "patriarchal." Once Jezebel was established in the church, this spirit began to usurp the things of God, stirring up sexual lust and immorality. The fear of the Lord and reverence for God departed and was replaced with a questioning of scripture and interminable discussions about the Bible.

The fruit of Jezebel in this church was an attack on the Bible, discouragement of godly believers, sexual fornication, homosexuality, adultery, pedophilia, abortion, divorce, imprisonment, and suicide. The church lost many mature believers and only began to recover when the minister moved on to another congregation elsewhere.

CASE STUDY FOUR

I have seen numerous people, both men and women, operating in the spirit of Jezebel. I have amalgamated several cases and developed a typical example of how the Jezebel spirit works.

Someone will join a church or organization and be most helpful and accommodating. They will gravitate towards the person in authority and be supportive and encouraging, often using flattery to appeal to the person's ego. They seek to quickly gain access to the leader's confidential affairs and work with them so that they soon become indispensable. The victim doesn't realize it, but the evil spirit has already begun to coil itself around them. As time passes, the Jezebel grows in influence in the leader's life. Suppose the Jezebel spirit is operating in a woman. In that case, she will be carefully looking for weaknesses and insecurities in the man, especially noting any marriage issues, and seeking to become his confidant, the person with whom he begins to share his problems with. The leader's wife will be the first to notice something wrong. She will usually sense that this new woman isn't a good influence around her husband, and they will begin to argue about her. The wife becomes critical of her husband, while the Jezebel supports and affirms him. The man further confides in his new "friend" and receives encouragement and admiration from her. Meanwhile, the man's wife continues to sense something is amiss and argues with her husband about the woman. The man becomes defensive of the woman, which further infuriates his wife. The couple's relationship becomes frosty, and they start to sleep in separate rooms.

If your spouse isn't giving you something you need, DO NOT accept it from anyone else.

The man takes solace in his ministry, which brings him into more contact with the Jezebel. A clear distinction has now evolved between home and work. At home, his wife has lost respect for him and is cold and critical. At work, the woman he's now promoted to his leadership team is warm, friendly, affirming, and full of admiration for him. The man spends more and more time at church with the woman who laughs at his jokes and thinks so highly of him. The Jezebel organizes work so that they frequently find themselves alone together. She begins to flirt with him, using flattery and seduction to boost his ego further and initiate a sexual encounter. Each day starts and ends with a hug in the office, then one day, it goes further, and adultery occurs. The man leaves his wife for the Jezebel. With her support, he continues in ministry, justifying his actions by saying that it was never God's will that he married his first wife and that the Lord has forgiven him. Now, he is free to marry this new woman, the one that God wanted him to marry all along.

This explanation may seem far-fetched, but I can't tell you how often I have heard such foolishness, even from senior leaders and elders. I also know of a church where the sex life in two marriages ceased. Hence, the woman from one marriage got together with the man from the other marriage and had a covert sexual relationship together. Everyone in the church knew about it but accepted it and never said anything. A Senior Elder told me this was common in that denomination, and as long as the couple was discrete, nobody, including the Pastor, thought it was wrong.

And we wonder why revival tarries.

OBSERVATIONS

The minister wasn't walking closely with the Lord as he should have been and became wide open to an attack from the enemy. He should have cultivated his relationship with God and his wife so that both were strong and stable. The way to a man's heart is through affirmation, and because he lacked understanding and character, the minister fell victim to the devil's plans for his life. His wife was correct to discern the Jezebel at work, but she wasn't listened to, due to her husband's insecurities and lack of wisdom. Ministers usually need help, support, and finances, but they should be careful about people's hidden agendas. Gift givers often expect favors from the recipient. Always be alert to entering into an unspoken "contract" with the giver. The minister should have discerned a Jezebel spirit when the woman started to give him something lacking at home. The married couple should have worked together to discuss and identify the Jezebel at work and taken measures to allow the minister's wife to work with her rather than her husband.

If your spouse isn't giving you something you need, DO NOT accept it from anyone else.

Go to the Lord in prayer, draw closer to Him, and He will help and support you. A married man must never work alone with a woman who is not his wife, and vice-versa. Even if no sexual sin is happening, it can appear as sin, and it may encourage others to behave in the same way, which could cause them to stumble.

Abstain from all appearance of evil.

1 Thessalonians 5:22 KJV

Men and women who spend time together alone become vulnerable to attack from demons of lust. Sin lurks at every door, and sexual immorality, especially in church leaders, is devastating. I know of two such leaders, God-fearing, Bible-believing men, who scorned the advice about spending time alone with other women and eventually fell into adultery. Ministers need to listen to their partners and work with them, never confiding in other people to the exclusion of their spouses. If there is a problem in your relationship, take time to sort things out together, and always be alert to people who negatively influence your marriage. I have seen couples torn apart, with women leaving husbands, men leaving wives, and then continuing in ministry with their new partners. Church leaders have told me that the Lord is OK with it, and they justify their evil behavior by saying that they realized that it was never God's will for them to be married to their first partner, so it isn't a sin to divorce them and marry someone else. Once this happens in the leadership, I have seen other couples in church suddenly decide to divorce and look for a new partner, following in the steps of the people they look up to. I have known a church where a minister's wife left her husband for another woman. Her husband resigned from his position, and his ex-wife became the minister with her lesbian partner. These are typical examples of the Jezebel spirit and are sadly all too common in our churches today.

And we wonder why revival tarries.

Chapter Twelve

GOD CREATED SEX

AND HE MAKES THE RULES

The collapse of biblical marriage precedes the collapse of society.

> ***Jesus said, "Have you not read that He who made them at the beginning 'made them male and female,' and said, 'For this reason a man shall leave his father and mother and be joined to his wife, and the two shall become one flesh'? So, they are no longer two, but one flesh. Therefore, what God has joined together, let no man put asunder."***
>
> **Matthew 19:4-6**

Sex is a gift from God for pleasure and procreation within marriage. God designed sex to occur within the sanctuary of a lifelong, exclusive marriage between a man and a woman. Through sexual intercourse, men and women become one person, and their lovemaking strengthens and nourishes their relationship. Sex in marriage is holy, good, and pleasing to the Lord. A married couple has a blessing from the Lord upon their marriage. If people remained faithful to their mate and only had sex within a Godly marriage, much pain and heartbreak would be avoided. Herpes, Syphilis, Gonorrhea, HIV, and Chlamydia would disappear. HIV and AIDS came about because of sexual immorality and was spread by the homosexual community. The Lord's design of a husband-and-wife partnership produces stable, healthy offspring where the whole family prospers. Restoring godly order within the home will see many of society's problems disappear. Politicians promise to establish law and order in the land, but if we returned to God's ways, we would have a peace and prosperity that can only be dreamed of.

Sexual experimentation before marriage is always a mistake and causes much heartache. We all want to find love and companionship, but we must trust that the one who made us knows what is best for us. The Lord wants us to be wise and make good choices in life. We will do well to trust His ways and not think we know best. The following verse is one to meditate on.

> ***Trust in the Lord with all your heart and lean not on your own understanding; in all your ways acknowledge Him, and He will direct your paths. Do not be wise in your own eyes; fear the Lord and depart from evil. It will be health to your body, and strength to your bones.***

Proverbs 3:5-8

God wants us to thrive in every area of our lives. A successful marriage is vital to our prosperity. It is essential to do things God's way and trust He knows what is best for us.

Men and women must guard their virginity until the Lord provides a mate for them. Courtship before marriage is an opportunity to get to know one another and assess your compatibility. Finding the Lord's will for your relationship is crucial before getting married. Spend time seeking the Lord until you get clear directions about marrying your prospective partner. God is a matchmaker; you can trust that He brings people together.

Do not entangle yourself sexually with the person before marriage, as this will cause you to become tied to the person prematurely, and it will become more challenging to hear from the Lord and receive guidance from Him. Do not date someone unless you are seriously considering marrying the person. Get to know them in social circles without spending time alone with them.

Politicians promise to establish law and order in the land, but if we returned to God's ways, we would have a peace and prosperity that can only be dreamed of.

Sexual behavior before marriage stifles the development of the relationship and masks potential problems you may have as a couple. Sexual intercourse is always wrong before marriage, as is getting too close physically to each other. Sin always gives a place to the devil in your life, which is the last thing you want when starting out in married life. Being too close physically will hinder your ability to know whether the person is right for you or not. I would say that once you are engaged, you can hold hands when walking down the street together, but it is best to leave kissing and hugging each other until you are married. I would balance this by saying that once the Lord has brought you your mate, you should marry them as soon as possible and begin your life together. It may not always be pleasing to the people around you, but getting married is a significant development away from the leadings of your parents. Family and friends can sometimes give us good advice, but we need to press into the Lord to discover what he wants for us and follow that lead, irrespective of how anyone else feels about it. When getting married, we need not conform to the cultural trends and expectations of those around us, including our families. People delay getting married because they are saving up for a lavish wedding or because it takes time to arrange for all the guests to be available on a specific date. Once you hear from the Lord about each other, it is best to get married quickly without the fanfare and cost that the world expects. If people can make the day, that's great; if they can't, bless them and do it anyway. I am not suggesting that we ignore all counsel and go against Godly advice, but we must be careful who we listen to. The opinions of those who love the Lord and who love both of you need to be listened to, but we must be selective when seeking advice from others. Listen to the Lord and hear from those mature in the faith and who have your best interest at heart.

Therefore, a man shall leave his father and mother and be joined to his wife, and they shall become one flesh.

Genesis 2:24

Jesus quoted this scripture in Matthew 19:4-6, affirming the scriptures to be valid from page one and emphasizing God's vision of marriage. Marriage is a profoundly spiritual experience that is difficult to describe. There is a mystery to Godly marriage that those who are on the outside cannot understand. God joins two people together physically and spiritually. Two people become one.

And He answered and said to them, "Have you not read that He who made them at the beginning 'made them male and female,' and said, 'For this reason a man shall leave his father and mother and be joined to his wife, and the two shall become one flesh'? So then, they are no longer two but one flesh. Therefore, what God has joined together, let not man separate."

Matthew 19:4-6

Marriage is when a man and a woman make a covenant of lifelong commitment to each other, exchanging solemn vows before God and man, and sex expresses their love. The institution of marriage provides a safe environment for this intimacy. God designed marriage to be the place where we can enjoy sex and raise a family. Marriage was God's idea, and He defined it to be a lasting union between a man and a woman.

Homosexual marriage is, therefore, contradictory to the definition of marriage as defined by the One who designed it. Marriage is between men and women. Same-sex couples can defy God and imitate a marriage ceremony, but it is an illegitimate union and contradictory to God's design of marriage, and it will not be blessed or recognized in heaven.

All sexual activity outside marriage between a man and a woman is sinful.

> ***Do you not know that the unrighteous will not inherit the kingdom of God? Do not be deceived. Neither the sexually immoral, nor idolaters, nor adulterers, nor male prostitutes, nor homosexuals, nor thieves, nor covetous, nor drunkards, nor revilers, nor extortioners will inherit the kingdom of God.***

1 Corinthians 6:9-10

Paul also quotes from Genesis 2:24

> ***"For this reason a man shall leave his father and mother and shall be joined to his wife, and the two shall be one flesh." This is a great mystery, but I am speaking about Christ and the church.***

Ephesians 5:31-32

There is a depth of mystery to marriage that cannot be explained. Marriage between a man and a woman with the Lord enthroned above them produces a three-way union of immense strength and spiritual significance.

> ***Marriage is to be honored among everyone, and the bed undefiled. But God will judge the sexually immoral and adulterers.***

Hebrews 13:4

SEXUAL SIN

The things of God only work when we do them His way.

All sexual activity outside marriage between a man and a woman is sinful. We turn from His ways at our peril. Sex outside of marriage produces instability and insecurity, with people becoming unfulfilled and unhappy.

Once you hear from the Lord about each other, it is best to get married quickly without the fanfare and cost that the world expects

We are free to break God's rules, but we have to face the consequences. Any deviation from biblical teaching is extremely dangerous. Sexual sin always gives the devil a place in your life, and he desires to bring pain and suffering to us.

> ***The thief does not come except to steal, and to kill, and to destroy. I have come that they may have life, and that they may have it more abundantly.***

John 10:10

Sexual sin invites demons into our lives, and their nature is to steal, kill, and destroy. Doing things God's way produces life and all good things, while going against the Lord's ways invites destruction.

> ***Flee sexual immorality. Every sin that a man does is outside the body, but he who commits sexual immorality sins against his own body.***

1 Corinthians 6:18 NKJV

Sexual sin is a grave danger; the Lord tells us to flee or run from it. Sinning sexually is as dangerous as entering the enclosure of a ferocious lion. We may not see it like that in the physical realm, but our lives are in danger spiritually. Don't go there, and if you find yourself in the vicinity of such sins, escape as quickly and urgently as possible.

The things of God only work when we do them His way.

The lips of an immoral woman drip as a honeycomb, and her mouth is smoother than oil. But her end is bitter as wormwood, sharp as a two-edged sword. Her feet go down to death. Remove your way far from her, and do not go near the door of her house, lest you give your honor to others, and your years to the cruel.

Proverbs 5:3-5 and 5:8-9

Flee from sexual sin!! As urgently and fearfully as you would flee from an enraged lion! The devil cares nothing for your pleasure and fun; he only uses sin to bring devastation into your life. A person who is enticed to commit sexual sin not only harms themselves but also brings devastation and destruction to their spouse and children. Satan will tempt you to sin, then stand back and gloat over the misery and heartbreak unfolding in your life. We need to learn to be self-controlled and deny the lust of the flesh.

Sexual immorality always allows demons to enter you

> ***Teaching us that, denying ungodliness and worldly lusts, we should live soberly, righteously, and godly, in this present world.***

Titus 2:12 KJV

Get wise to the devil's ways and choose life instead. Find contentment with your mate instead of allowing the devil to multiply cravings and dissatisfaction in you. Stay on the path of life and trust in the Lord and His ways with all your heart and understanding.

> ***I urge you therefore, brothers, by the mercies of God, that you present your bodies as a living sacrifice, holy, and acceptable to God, which is your reasonable service of worship.***

Romans 12:1

Satan leads people astray to gain control over them so that he can harm them and then use them to wreak havoc everywhere they go. Sexual sin spreads like a virus. People fall into sin, and the devil gains a foothold in their lives. Sexual immorality always allows demons to enter you, and then these demons lead you into more sin, enabling evil spirits to spread from person to person. Stop the spread of this spiritual plague by turning back to Christ, repenting of sinful lifestyles, and commanding all demons that came into you to leave in Jesus's name.

Satan breaks hearts wherever he goes. Stop sinning and keep him out of your life.

Humble yourself under God's Word and flee sexual immorality. The devil is not interested in our sexual pleasure but in our sexual sin. Sexual sin is one of Satan's most powerful weapons. He tempts people with discontent and thoughts of lust and sexual desire. The devil will send people into your life to entice you into sin and lead you astray. We need to each walk closely with the Lord and be vigilant against the many schemes of the devil.

Lest Satan should take advantage of us. For we are not ignorant of his devices.

2 Corinthians 2:11

Our enemies are the devil and his demons. We are forever against them, as they are against us. It is a fight to the death without mercy or forgiveness. It is, however, different with people. Other people may oppose us and even harm us significantly, but each human has a precious soul that needs to be saved. We bless those who curse us and pray for those who spitefully use us, hoping they, too, will repent and accept Jesus as their Lord and Savior.

For our fight is not against flesh and blood, but against principalities, against powers, against the rulers of the darkness of this world, and against spiritual forces of evil in the heavenly places.

Ephesians 6:12

We need to be generously merciful and forgiving towards all people, hoping that some will be saved, knowing that unless they choose Jesus, they will spend an eternity in Hell.

Do you not know that the unrighteous will not inherit the kingdom of God? Do not be deceived. Neither

fornicators, nor idolaters, nor adulterers, nor homosexuals, nor sodomites.

1 Corinthians 6:9

Those who live a lifestyle of homosexuality, adultery, and sex outside of marriage have no place in God's kingdom. They are rebels under the headship of the lord of the rebels, who is the devil. Living in active sin desensitizes us to the leadership of the Holy Spirit. We become filled with darkness and puffed up with pride and begin to lose sight of right and wrong, of what is holy and what is unholy.

Those who live a lifestyle of homosexuality, adultery, and sex outside of marriage have no place in God's kingdom.

Woe to those who call evil good, and good evil; who exchange darkness for light, and light for darkness; who exchange bitter for sweet, and sweet for bitter!

Isaiah 5:20

At first, people feel guilty and know they are sinning, but their conscience becomes distorted as time passes and will eventually stop working altogether.

Now the Spirit clearly says that in the last times some will depart from the faith and pay attention to seducing spirits and doctrines of devils, speaking lies in hypocrisy, having their consciences seared with a hot iron,

1 Timothy 4:1-2

Jesus always tells the truth. We may not like it or agree with it, but truth is truth. Jesus said in John 14:6 that," I am the Way, the Truth, and the Life, and no one comes to the Father except through Me." Your feelings and conscience must be submitted to God's Word. Emotions and desires can be deceptive, and human reasoning can become misguided. You must humble yourself before God's Word and accept that the Lord is right. Even when you don't understand it, even when it doesn't feel right.

There is a way that seems right to a man, but its end is the way of death.

Proverbs 14:12

This I say, therefore, and testify in the Lord, that you should no longer walk as the rest of the Gentiles walk, in the futility of their mind, having their understanding darkened, being alienated from the life of God, because of the ignorance that is in them, because of the blindness of their heart;

who, being past feeling, have given themselves over to lewdness, to work all uncleanness with greediness.

Ephesians 4:17-19

The influences and cultural trends around us easily distort our thinking and feelings. Your reasoning, thoughts, and emotions are not foolproof. Each day, we all need to be washed and refreshed with the clean waters of God's Word so that our moral compass stays aligned with God's Word.

Do not be conformed to this world, but be transformed by the renewing of your mind, that you may prove what is the good and acceptable and perfect will of God.

Romans 12:2

God is not a liar. His Word is His bond, and it cannot be broken. You may try to break God's Word, but God's Word will end up breaking you.

The entirety of Your word is truth, and every one of Your righteous judgments endures forever.

Psalm 119:160

God says what He means and means what He says. He is so sure of His Words that He wrote them down. Jesus said in Mark 13:31

"heaven and earth will pass away, but My Words will never pass away."

Mark 13:31

The whole universe was created when Jesus spoke it into being, and it will continue until He speaks the last Word, and then it will cease to exist. The only thing that will survive the ending of heaven and earth will be our souls and the Word of God. Every person who claims that the Bible doesn't mean what it says about sexual immorality is deluded.

All sexual behavior outside of marriage between a man and a woman is sin.

You may disagree with the Bible, or claim that it should have been written differently, but the text consistently states that homosexuality is sinful behavior. The principal sin in Sodom was homosexuality. Not rape, lack of hospitality, or sex outside of marriage. These things have happened throughout the history of the world, yet God didn't judge them by sending fire from heaven. Sodom was destroyed because all the men, young and old, were completely sold out to a homosexual lifestyle, and this was an abomination to the Lord. A study of Genesis 19 with cross-references confirms this, and it would be incorrect to suggest otherwise.

But before they retired for the night, all the men of Sodom, young and old, came from all over the city and surrounded the house. They shouted to Lot, "Where are the men who came to

spend the night with you? Bring them out to us so we can have sex with them!"

Genesis 19:4-5 NLT

Don't forget the cities of Sodom and Gomorrah and their neighboring towns, all full of lust of every kind, including lust of men for other men. Those cities were destroyed by fire and continue to be a warning to us that there is a hell in which sinners are punished. Yet these false teachers carelessly go right on living their evil, immoral lives, degrading their bodies, and laughing at those in authority over them, even scoffing at the Glorious Ones.

Jude 1: 7-8

He condemned the cities of Sodom and Gomorrah to destruction by reducing them to ashes, making them an example to those afterward who would live ungodly lives; and if He delivered righteous Lot, who was distressed by the filthy conduct of the wicked for that righteous man lived among them, and what he saw and heard of their lawless deeds tormented his righteous soul day after day.

2 Peter 2:6-8

You may disagree with the Bible, which you are free to do so, but God will have the last word. It would be wise to heed His Word now and make your peace with Him before that terrible day when we will all stand before the judgment seat of Christ.

> ***For we must all appear before the judgment seat of Christ, that each one may receive his recompense in the body, according to what he has done, whether it was good or bad.***

2 Corinthians 5:10

God's opinion is the only one that matters. Everyone must humble themselves before His thinking, knowing God is righteous in all things and always right. We may need help to understand what He says in His Word, and we may not always like it or agree with it, but God knows best. He is always right and can be trusted.

> ***For My thoughts are not your thoughts, nor are your ways My ways, says the Lord. For as the heavens are higher than the earth, so are My ways higher than your ways, and My thoughts than your thoughts.***

Isaiah 55:8-9

God's Word is unequivocal about homosexuality.

> ***You shall not lie with a man as one does with a woman. It is an abomination.***

Leviticus 18:22

People who interpret the Bible to suit their own ideas are heading for destruction.

> ***Be not deceived. God is not mocked. For whatever a man sows, that will he also reap.***
>
> **Galatians 6:7**

You need to be led by God's Word and not by your own ideas and reasonings. The Bible is a sure foundation to build your life on, but an unmovable object when you push against it. You will be wise to agree with God and align yourself with the immovable rock of His Word.

> ***Whoever hears these sayings of Mine and does them, I will liken him to a wise man who built his house on a rock.***
>
> **Matthew 7:24**

In the light of these scriptures, I counsel you to humble yourself before the truth of the Bible while you still have the opportunity to do so. Jesus is reaching out to you in love, hoping that you say yes to Him. God isn't expecting you to become perfect before entering into relationship with Him, but He yearns for you to open up your heart and accept His forgiveness and friendship.

Chapter Thirteen

LEAVE THE BOTTLE OF SIN OUTSIDE

SERVING GOD ON HIS TERMS NOT OURS

let us also lay aside every weight and the sin that so easily entangles us and let us run with endurance the race that is set before us. Let us look to Jesus, the author and finisher of our faith, who for the joy that was set before Him endured the cross, despising the shame, and is seated at the right hand of the throne of God.

Hebrew 12:1-2

We cannot serve two masters. We cannot serve Jesus and serve another at the same time. We have to choose whom we will serve. Many people today want the benefits of following God but don't want to leave their self-serving lifestyle behind. They call Jesus "God", but then follow their own feelings and desires, deluding themselves into thinking that God will go along with their reasoning.

> ***Jesus does NOT expect you to sort your life out before becoming a Christian,***

> ***For My thoughts are not your thoughts, nor are your ways My ways, says the Lord. For as the heavens are higher than the earth, so are My ways higher than your ways, and My thoughts than your thoughts.***
>
> **Isaiah 55:8-9**

To illustrate this point, let me share an encounter that happened many years ago while working in a homeless shelter. We would temporarily take people in off the street until we could find housing for them. One winters night, a man was sitting on the pavement outside. The weather was terrible; he was soaking wet and freezing to death. When we invited him in, we noticed he was clutching a bottle of wine. We said he could shower, have a change clothes, a hot meal, and somewhere to sleep for the night, but he would have to leave the bottle of wine outside. The man desperately wanted to come in but started arguing with us about his wine. He refused to leave his alcohol outside. We tried talking to him, but he insisted on bringing his wine with him. Sadly, with heaviness of heart, we had to close the door on him because he refused to comply with our conditions, and he remained outside.

This sad story reflects where many people are today. They want to come into God's kingdom, but on their terms. They want to indulge their sin while enjoying all the benefits of heaven. God is a Great King, the King of Kings, and He has a Kingdom. He desperately wants everyone to come in and enjoy His Kingdom, but we must comply with his conditions. The homeless man wanted to come into the hostel, but he insisted on coming in on his terms, and maybe died that night as a consequence. We didn't ask him to have a wash, clean himself up, change his clothes, or even pay money, but the condition was that no alcohol was allowed in the center. So it is with God's kingdom. Jesus does NOT expect you to sort your life out before becoming a Christian, but you do need to humble yourselves before God and admit your need of a Savior. The Lord wants to come into your life and work with you as your loving Father, patiently dealing with issues and working through problems one at a time.

> ***You cannot drink the cup of the Lord and the cup of demons. You cannot be partakers of the Lord's table and of the table of demons.***

1 Corinthians 10:21

Sadly, many people today are arguing with the Lord and trying to reason with Him about the rules of His Kingdom. They are attempting to break God's Word but will end up destroying themselves.

> ***There is a way that seems right to a man, but its end is the way of death.***

Proverbs 14:12

God is not a tyrant who is there to frustrate us. He loves every person and wants to welcome us into His Kingdom, where we will be cleaned up and cared for. However, we must enter through the doorway of humility and repentance and submit to the master of the house. People are rebellious, and the reality is that only those who do things God's way will be able to have a relationship with the Father.

Do not deceive yourself into thinking you can have a relationship with God while holding onto a rebellious lifestyle. We cannot serve two masters. Inevitably, we will hate one and love the other. Since the beginning of time, men and women have desired to walk with God while walking in rebellion to Him at the same time.

However, the things of God only work when we do them His way.

You are not defined by your sexuality or the choices you have made in life. We were each made in God's image, but we have all been marred by the Fall of Man and become distorted. We may decide to dishonor God by the choices we make in life, but we are still intrinsically of great value to Him. Every person who has ever lived is worth more than the whole earth and everything within it.

Jesus came to suffer the agony of the cross so that every person can have peace with God. If you were the only person who lived on the earth, Jesus would still have come down from heaven and died for you. Regardless of what you have done or who you are. When Jesus died on the cross, every sin that has, or that ever could be committed, was dealt with and forgiven.

Jesus told a story about a man who became dissatisfied with life. He rejected his father, took his inheritance, and left home. He lived a lifestyle of self-indulgence until all his money was spent, and then found himself living with pigs and desperately unhappy. After some time, the man realized the error of his ways and wanted to go home to his father. He realized that he was no longer fit to be called his son, but he wondered if it may be possible to be his servant. As soon as the man left the pigs to return home, his father saw him, ran, and hugged him. The boy began explaining that he wasn't fit to be his son but maybe could be a servant. His father, however, began rejoicing, saying that his son had come home.

Then He said: "A certain man had two sons. And the younger of them said to his father, 'Father, give me the portion of goods that falls to me.' So, he divided to them his livelihood. And not many days after, the younger son gathered all together, journeyed to a far country, and there wasted his possessions with prodigal living. But when he had spent all, there arose a severe famine in that land, and he began to be in want. Then he went and joined himself to a citizen of that country, and he sent him into his fields to feed swine. And he would gladly have filled his stomach with the pods that the swine ate, and no one gave him anything. "But when he came to himself, he said, 'How many of my father's hired servants have bread enough and to spare, and I perish with hunger! I will arise and go to my father, and will say to him, "Father, I have sinned against heaven and before you, and I am no longer worthy to be called your son. Make me like one of your hired servants."' "And he arose and came to his father. But when he was still a great way off, his father saw him and had compassion, and ran and fell on his neck and kissed him. And the son said to him, 'Father, I have sinned against heaven and in your sight, and am no longer worthy to be called your

> ***son.' "But the father said to his servants, 'Bring out the best robe and put it on him and put a ring on his hand and sandals on his feet. And bring the fatted calf here and kill it and let us eat and be merry; for this my son was dead and is alive again; he was lost and is found.' And they began to be merry.***

Luke 15:11-24

Jesus's story about the man and his father illustrates our relationship with God. We have become separated from God by our sins. God respects our free will and patiently waits for us to return home. When we reflect on our choices and behavior, we realize the error of our ways and decide to come back to God. We return in a different spirit, letting go of pride and self-will. We now want to serve rather than be served. To be obedient rather than rebellious and self-willed. We will now submit to God's ways rather than dictate to God how we think things should be done. We all have the same problem, whether we admit it or not. We are full of sin and out of relationship with God. Each of us has fallen short of God's standards and become separated from Him.

> ***If we say that we have no sin, we deceive ourselves, and the truth is not in us. If we confess our sins, he is faithful and just to forgive us our sins, and to cleanse us from all unrighteousness.***

1 John 1:8-9 KJV

Whether we realize it or not, we all yearn to be close to God. All of us have a deep need that can only be satisfied by being in a relationship with our creator. God, however, is a Holy God, and only perfect, holy people can be close to Him. No person in themselves will ever be good enough for God, no matter how many good things they do in this life. Every one of us has inherited the nature of Adam, which is the nature of a rebel. We are all destined to be separated from Him forever due to our rebellion. Every one of us rightly deserves to be separated from God. We are deserving of death. Yet God, in His love for us, found a way for this punishment to be placed on to someone who did not deserve death. Jesus came to offer Himself to die in place of us.

We become free from the penalty of sin when we believe in Jesus Christ, and He becomes our Lord. Jesus deals with our separation from God when we believe in and accept what He accomplished for us on the cross.

To be forgiven for our sins and enter into a relationship with God, we must first agree with Him about the definition of sin, as stated in the Bible. All other interpretations of sin are incorrect and will be useless to you.

We admit to God that we deserve to be separated from Him and ask for forgiveness. We accept the perfect work of the cross, where Jesus died, and those who believe in Him have the death they deserve credited to them by Jesus's death. This means we are now free from judgment and can have a relationship with God.

Let me again stress that God loves you. It is crucial to meditate on this truth and receive it. Without knowing that God loves you, it becomes difficult to receive forgiveness, to believe that God will heal you, and to have any meaningful relationship with Him. The Lord is not your boss; He is your Father. You are not an employee; you are His son or daughter.

Doubting that God loves you gives Satan an open doorway into your life to afflict you with shame, discouragement, and despair. God's love enables faith and belief to be built in our lives, which then opens the door to receiving all that we need from Him.

We must know God's love.

We can then rest in God's love.

His love is the foundation stone of our hope.

He cannot love you more than He does.

His love is not conditional.

It cannot be earned.

He does not love you more when you do good things and less when you sin. His love for you is a constant and irrefutable reality.

God is for you, not against you.

You are valuable and so precious to Him.

He wants to be in a relationship with you.

We are all loved, and we are all important to Him.

He loves you so much that He was prepared to allow Jesus to suffer and be killed so that we could be with Him.

> ***For God was in Christ, reconciling the world to himself, no longer counting people's sins against them. And he gave us this wonderful message of reconciliation.***

2 Corinthians 5:19

He loves you so much that He would still have come and died for you, even if you were the only person in the world.

> ***This is good and pleases God our Savior, who wants everyone to be saved and to understand the truth.***
>
> **1 Timothy 2:3-4**

God loves all people and desires everyone to know Him and accept His means of salvation.

God loves homosexuals.

God loves adulterers.

God loves pedophiles.

God loves Satanists.

God loves murderers.

The Lord is not your boss; He is your Father.

God loves those who hate Him.

God loves every person.

God loves you.

Whoever you are.

Whatever you have done.

Whatever has been done to you.

Whatever you feel about yourself.

God wants to heal you.

God has good plans for you.

God wants to prosper you.

God sees a great future for you.

God is not waiting for you to become holy before you reach out to Him.

He wants you to come to Him now, as you are, and He will begin the restoration process in your life.

The Bible says that Christ died for us before we were worthy to be saved.

> ***But God showed his great love for us by sending Christ to die for us while we were still sinners.***

Romans 5:8

God loves us before we clean our lives up.

Before we get things in order.

Before we feel good enough for God.

> ***If you are willing and obedient you will eat the good of the land.***

Isaiah 1:19

If we willingly submit to God's ways and obey His Word, we will prosper in body, soul, mind, and spirit.

However, the truth is that the promises of God are all conditional. The way back to Him is by admitting our sins and returning with a different attitude to do things God's way rather than our way.

It is time to sit down and think about our lives and decide whether we should return to the Father.

And like the prodigal son, we must humble ourselves and carefully consider how we will return.

Chapter Fourteen

DELIVERANCE

HOW DEMONS GAIN ACCESS TO OUR LIVES AND HOW TO GET RID OF THEM

> ***whosoever shall call on the name of the Lord shall be delivered.***

Joel 2:32 KJV

As an introduction to this chapter, I want to make the following statement. Satan is a defeated foe.

People can get all excited about the devil, but it is essential to know that the battle was won by Jesus on the cross 2,000 years ago.

> ***And having disarmed authorities and powers, He made a show of them openly, triumphing over them by the cross.***

Colossians 2:15

The devil's biggest fear is that we discover who we are in Christ and what authority we have been given. Satan cannot stand against a Christian who realizes who they are and then tells him to stop what he is doing and leave. We use our authority, in the name of Jesus, and demons have to flee from us. Satan has no power over us. He was terminally defeated by the Lord Jesus Christ at the cross and was stripped of his authority. Satan knows what he is, but he wants to see if we know what he is, and until he sees that, he will try to exert an illegitimate authority over us.

> ***For this purpose, the Son of God was revealed that He might destroy the works of the devil.***

1 John 3:8

Most spiritual warfare does not involve face-offs with demons. Spiritual warfare is usually fought in the mind. The greatest spiritual battle we will ever face is our daily battle to maintain a relationship with the Lord in prayer and Bible study. Bearing this in mind, let's have a look at deliverance.

> ***Then war broke out in heaven. Michael and his angels fought against the dragon, and the dragon and his angels fought, but they did not prevail, nor was there a place for them in heaven any longer. The great dragon was cast out, that ancient serpent called the Devil and Satan, who deceives the whole world. He was cast down to the earth, and his angels were cast down with him.***

Revelation 12:7-9

Satan and a third of the angels rebelled against God and were subsequently thrown out of heaven. These angels became demons. They are utterly evil and opposed to God and humanity. They are the "spiritual hosts" spoken of in Ephesians 6:12.

For we do not wrestle against flesh and blood, but against principalities, against powers, against the rulers of the darkness of this age, against spiritual hosts of wickedness in the heavenly places.

Ephesians 6:12

We do not know how many there are, we know that there are twice as many angels than demons, but how many we don't know. I assume that the word "hosts" means a vast army of demons arrayed against us today.

The devil's biggest fear is that we discover who we are in Christ and what authority we have been given.

Demons do the bidding of their master, Satan, opposing God and humanity. Satan has a kingdom that he rules. He gets no credit for his organized kingdom; he copied the structures of God's kingdom in heaven and arrays his demons in ordered ranks and hierarchy.

Sin allows demons to grow in influence over people and sometimes to enter into them, where they become much more effective in persuading them to do their bidding. Demons are spirits without bodies, and they constantly crave inhabiting humans so they can be much more active in this world.

God has limited Himself and Satan to work through humans in this world. People have free will, and Satan is not allowed to do whatever he wants to in the world. He must influence and operate through people. This is why he invests so much time and effort in getting us to sin, because when we sin, we give place to the devil, and he grows in influence in our lives.

Be angry, but do not sin. Do not let the sun go down on your anger. Do not give place to the devil.

Ephesians 4:26-27

Once a demon gains access to a person, he will stay there if he wants to, or until the person dies; at this point, he departs the dead body and enters a close relative as part of that person's inheritance. In some cultures, such as American Indians, they sometimes make a will of their worldly goods and a list of their demons as to who will receive them. Inherited demons are the spiritual power in a generational curse. For example, a person sins by committing adultery; consequently, a demon of sexual immorality enters them. The person will now find it much harder to resist committing further sexual sin because the temptation to sin is no longer coming at them from the outside; it is from the demon who now lives inside them.

When that person dies, the demon will enter one of their offspring, and they, in turn, will be led into adultery and sexual sin. This is why we see patterns of sinful behavior such as alcoholism, abuse, and perversion recurring from one generation to the next. It usually worsens with each generation as they accumulate more demons. People learn to manage the demons in them, but the evil spirits still exert significant influence over them.

CASE STUDY ONE: DEMONIC INFLUENCE

Many years ago, I was involved in a deliverance with a Christian man living an openly sinful lifestyle. The Church he was involved with was liberal, and consequently, the man had been encouraged to live in sexual sin, amongst other things. Thankfully, the Lord got a hold of him, and he realized that he needed to come back to God and repent from his sinful lifestyle. He did this, and he was delivered from multiple demons. One of the things that changed in him after he was delivered was losing his attitude toward antisemitism. He said that whenever Israel was mentioned or the Jews, he used to immediately react negatively. He would denounce Israel and hear nothing good about her people. He said there was an emotional response when the Jews were mentioned, not a reasoned response, and he could not discuss or be open to hearing any positive opinion about them. After he was delivered from demons, one of the behaviors that changed was that he suddenly realized that the Jews are God's people and that the Lord had given the land of Israel to the Jewish people. It was as if his eyes had been opened to the injustice and hatred the world manifests towards Israel, and he now had a love for them, and could see that the Bible has much to say about blessing them.

when we sin, we give place to the devil, and he grows in influence in our lives.

This was an example of how demons can cause an unreasonable reaction to the things of God. I see demonic influence throughout society, in rebellious groups such as Marxism, Antifa, and Black Lives Matter, as well as the increase in sexual deviance. Demons will always be against the purposes of God and will always lead the person into further sinful activities. The only thing that breaks this cycle is when a person gives their life to the Lord Jesus Christ, and a Christian uses their authority and commands the demons to leave the person. By the time Jesus was ministering in Israel 2,000 years ago, the people had lived ungodly lives for thousands of years. Demons had gained access to so many of them that when Jesus and His disciples started ministering, they were inundated by people who needed deliverance from evil spirits.

> ***That evening after sunset, the people brought to Jesus all the sick and demon possessed. The whole town gathered at the door, and Jesus healed many who had various diseases. He also drove out many demons, but he would not let the demons speak because they knew who he was.***

Mark 1:32-34.

> ***When evening came, many who were demon-possessed were brought to him, and he drove out the spirits with a word and healed all the sick***

Matthew 8:16

Deuteronomy 28 tells us that there are devastating consequences to sin. Was this ever revoked? Do we assume that because we accepted Christ and received salvation, all the demons in us have been removed? Where is the scriptural evidence for this?

> ***Do not be deceived, God is not mocked; for whatever a man sows, that he will also reap.***

Galatians 6:7

Sin weakens our relationship with Jesus, and some sins permit demon spirits to enter us. Sins that always allow demons to come into us include all sexual immorality, any involvement in the occult, drug use, drunkenness, and the practice of false religions. The following verse shows us that after we become Christians, we still need to cleanse our lives. Paul was writing to the believers in Corinth.

> ***Therefore, having these promises, beloved, let us cleanse ourselves from all filthiness of the flesh and spirit, perfecting holiness in the fear of God.***

2 Corinthians 7:1

Demons are filthy and evil. We invited them into our lives when we chose to sin, and we need to systematically confess our sins to God and then tell all demons that came into us through our sins to get out, in Jesus' name. The spirit realm works as one vast legal system. For example, if a demon temps us to sin sexually and we go on to break God's law, the protective wall around us is compromised, and a demon has the legal right to enter us.

> ***He who digs a pit will fall into it, and whoever breaks through a wall will be bitten by a serpent.***

Ecclesiastes 10:8

We read about God's people who sinned in the Bible. The spiritual wall of protection was removed, and demons were able to come in and devastate the land.

> ***So now I will tell you what I will do to My vineyard: I will take away its hedge, and it shall be consumed; I will break down its wall, and it shall be trodden down.***

Isaiah 5:5

See, I will send serpents against you, adders, which will not be charmed, and they will bite you, declares the Lord.

Jeremiah 8:17

Conversely, we are forgiven when we confess our sins to God and turn from our sinful lifestyles.

If we confess our sins, He is faithful and just to forgive us our sins and to cleanse us from all unrighteousness.

1 John 1:9

When we admit our sins to the Lord, we instantly benefit from the forgiveness that He gave us at the cross. This means that spiritually, we have claimed back the legal right to be free from demons, and we can then use our authority and demand that they leave us in Jesus' name, and all demons will have to depart from us. We have taken back our legal rights over our lives by dealing with our sins. Once we have the legal rights over the demons, we can command them to leave in Jesus's name. It is now easy to order them to go, and they must do so.

Addressing your sinful lifestyle is the key to your deliverance.

Please don't give your front door key to a thief because he will come in and rob you blind. SINNING IS GIVING YOUR KEY TO THE DEVIL. Christians cannot continue in sin and expect to prevail against the devil. Satan will defeat us and steal everything he gets his claws on. We need to not only admit our sins but repent from them as well. Repentance means STOP DOING IT!

You cannot drink the cup of the Lord and the cup of demons. You cannot be

partakers of the Lord's table and of the table of demons.

1 Corinthians 10:21

You adulterers and adulteresses, do you not know that the friendship with the world is enmity with God? Whoever therefore will be a friend of the world is the enemy of God.

submit yourselves to God. Resist the devil, and he will flee from you. Draw near to God, and He will draw near to you. Cleanse your hands, you sinners, and purify your hearts, you double-minded.

James 4:4 and 4:7-8

There was, and still is, a pandemic of demons dwelling in people, and we, as Christians, are called to deal with them. We are:

God's 'pest control force.'

Getting rid of these spiritual vermin.

Preaching the gospel.

Making disciples wherever we go.

Do we still have demons in people today? One look at modern life tells us that we live in an increasingly lawless society, and consequently, there will be at least as many demonized people around us if not many more than in Jesus's time.

> ***He said to them, "Go into all the world and preach the gospel to every creature. He who believes and is baptized will be saved. But he who does not believe will be condemned. These signs will accompany those who believe: In My name they will cast out demons; they will speak with new tongues; they will take up serpents; if they drink any deadly thing, it will not hurt them; they will lay hands on the sick, and they will recover." After the Lord had spoken to them, He was received up into heaven and sat at the right hand of God. Then they went forth and preached everywhere, the Lord working with them and confirming the word through the accompanying signs. Amen.***

Mark 16:15-20

Jesus sent His disciples out to do these things: cast out demons, heal the sick, and preach the kingdom. I notice that their ministry to people often began with casting out demons.

> ***Then He called His twelve disciples together and gave them power and authority over all demons, and to cure diseases. He sent them to preach the kingdom of God and to heal the sick.***

Luke 9:1-2

After this, the Lord appointed seventy others and sent them two by two ahead of Him into every city and place where He Himself was about to come.

Luke 10:1

The seventy returned with joy, saying, "Lord, even the demons are subject to us through Your name." He said to them, "I saw Satan as lightning fall from heaven. Look, I give you authority to trample on serpents and scorpions, and over all the power of the enemy. And nothing shall by any means hurt you. Nevertheless, do not rejoice that the spirits are subject to you, but rather rejoice that your names are written in heaven."

Luke 10:17

At evening, when the sun had set, they brought to Him all who were sick and those who were demon-possessed. And the whole city was gathered together at the door. Then He healed many who were sick with various diseases and cast out many demons; and He did not allow the demons to speak, because they knew Him.

Mark 1:32-34

Deliverance and healing were not seen as something added to the preaching of the Word; deliverance and healing the sick often preceded the preaching, and it certainly was at the heart of the ministry of the Word.

In Luke 10:17, the disciples reported to Jesus that they had been casting demons out of people as part of their ministry. Clearly, deliverance was an integral part of the disciples' work as they went out to preach the word. I conclude that if dealing with demons was so necessary at that time, it must be even more critical today because we live in such ungodly times. One of the last things Jesus said to His followers before He returned to heaven was that they were to cast demons out of people.

Addressing your sinful lifestyle is the key to your deliverance.

> ***And these signs will follow those who believe: In My name they will cast out demons.***

Mark 16:17

Then we read that the disciples went out and ministered in the way they had seen and been taught by Jesus to minister, which included preaching the gospel and casting demons out of people.

> ***And they went out and preached everywhere, the Lord working with them and confirming the word through the accompanying signs.***

Mark 16:20

The signs that accompanied their preaching were casting demons out of people, healing the sick, speaking in tongues, and raising the dead; miracles and prophetic ministry were thrown in as well.

Demons cannot simply jump into people. We all have a God-given protection around us that demons cannot break through. Even unbelievers have this to some degree. However, we compromise our protection from demons through our sinful lifestyles and ignorance of how demons gain access to us through generational lines of inheritance.

> ***my people are gone into captivity,***
> ***because they have no knowledge:***

Isaiah 5:13 KJV

> ***My people perish for lack of knowledge.***

Hosea 4:6

When we accepted Jesus as our Lord and Savior, we received the Holy Spirit and qualified for all the benefits Jesus won for us at the cross. We should have all been punished and killed for our sins, but God, in His love, sent His Son Jesus to suffer on the cross in every way we deserved. God loved us so much that he was willing to pay the price in His own body so that when we believe and accept Jesus as our Lord, we are credited with serving our sentence because Jesus has already suffered it on our behalf. God Himself died for us.

> ***take heed to yourselves and to the entire flock, over which the Holy Spirit has made you overseers, to shepherd the church of God which He purchased with His own blood.***

Acts 20:28

This deal is the most fantastic in the history of existence. The death and separation from God that we rightly deserve, our deserved sentence, was served by God Himself so that by believing in Him, we receive complete forgiveness and all the benefits Christ Himself enjoys.

> ***Blessed be the God and Father of our Lord Jesus Christ, who has blessed us with every spiritual blessing in the heavenly places in Christ,***

Ephesians 1:3

> ***He raised us up and seated us together in the heavenly places in Christ Jesus, so that in the coming ages He might show the surpassing riches of His grace in kindness toward us in Christ Jesus. For by grace you have been saved through faith, and this is not of yourselves. It is the gift of God, not of works, so that no one should boast.***

Ephesians 2:6-10

When we say "Yes" to Jesus, we access the forgiveness and blessing that Jesus won for us 2,000 years ago on the cross. God has established us as holy and perfect in His sight. We are now as righteous as Jesus is. This is the magnificence, glory, and spectacular victory of the cross; God has seated us with Christ in heaven, where we receive the same blessings that Jesus enjoys.

> ***Surely, He has borne our grief and carried our sorrows; Yet we esteemed Him stricken, smitten of God, and***

afflicted. But He was wounded for our transgressions, He was bruised for our iniquities; the chastisement of our peace was upon Him, and by His stripes we are healed.

Isaiah 53:4-5

Jesus suffered and died so that we don't have to. By believing in Him, we receive peace with God, and the works of the devil are forever destroyed in our lives. We now have the favor and blessing of God resting on us. Our sins have been forgiven, even the ones we haven't committed yet, and every sickness has been healed. When God Himself died on the cross, when Jesus died, He generated vast reservoirs of forgiveness and healing. He provided enough forgiveness for every sin that will ever be committed, and enough healing for every sickness that will ever exist. So much forgiveness and healing was generated by the perfect work of the cross, that if every person received all the forgiveness and healing they needed, there would still be an ocean of forgiveness and healing left over. Jesus gave you these free gifts of forgiveness and healing when He endured the agony of the cross. You can receive these undeserved gifts by believing in Him. God ruled in your favor 2,000 years ago, and He will not change His mind. Jesus loves you and wants to help you.

The Lord is not slow concerning His promise, as some count slowness. But He is patient with us, because He does not want any to perish, but all to come to repentance.

2 Peter 3:9

For the wages of sin is death, but the gift of God is eternal life through Jesus Christ our Lord.

Romans 6:23

God has already decided to forgive your sins and heal you from every illness. He is saying yes to your requests! We must believe and receive the Lord's gifts and thank Him. To disbelieve this is to deny the Lord and His good intentions towards us. It is disrespectful and insulting to the Lord when we doubt He has forgiven and healed us. We must humbly accept God's free gifts and receive them with thanksgiving.

We are now as righteous as Jesus is.

Bless the Lord, O my soul, and forget not all His benefits, who forgives all your iniquities, who heals all your diseases, who redeems your life from the pit, who crowns you with lovingkindness and tender mercies, who satisfies your mouth with good things, so that your youth is renewed like the eagle's.

Psalm 103:2-5

As far as the east is from the west, so far has He removed our transgressions from us.

Psalm 103:12

Jesus stated in Matthew 7:13 that many people will go to Hell, but they will die and spend an eternity in damnation, forgiven for all their sins. The reason they will be thrown into eternal suffering is not because they were unforgiven; it is because they rejected Jesus as their Lord and Savior. Why do we suffer from sickness and disease today? It's not because God hasn't healed us. Jesus has done all the healing He is ever going to do. Our unbelief keeps us from receiving all that Jesus won for us at Calvary. God eradicated pain, illness, and premature death at the cross, but we don't walk in the victory Jesus died to give us because we don't believe. The problem is with us, not with God. He has healed us; we need to study the scriptures and learn how to receive His healing. We need to confess our sins to God, not to be forgiven, but to be removed from the consequences of our sins. Deuteronomy 28 tells us that there are devastating consequences to sin. Was this ever revoked? Do we assume that because we accepted Christ and received salvation, all the demons in us have been removed? Where is the scriptural evidence for this?

Jesus has done all the healing He is ever going to do.

> ***I call heaven and earth to witness against you this day that I have set before you life and death, blessing and curse. Therefore choose life, that both you and your descendants may live.***

Deuteronomy 30:19

God has given us the gift of free will, and He will honor and respect our decisions. The decisions we make in this life will decide where we spend eternity. We will live forever in Heaven with the Lord or in Hell in endless agony, and we can choose which one. The following verse shows us that after we become Christians, we still need to cleanse our lives. Paul was addressing this instruction to the believers in Corinth, to those who were in the church.

> ***Therefore, having these promises, beloved, let us cleanse ourselves from all filthiness of the flesh and spirit, perfecting holiness in the fear of God.***

2 Corinthians 7:1

Demons are filthy and evil. We invited them into our lives when we chose to sin, and we need to systematically confess our sins to God and then tell all demons that came into us through our sins to get out, in Jesus's name. The reason that demons tempt us to sin is so that they can gain a place in our lives. Many Christians today do not believe in demons, and those who do often think they cannot inhabit a Christian. These erroneous teachings come directly from Satan himself.

> ***Now the Holy Spirit tells us clearly that in the last times some will turn away from the true faith; they will follow deceptive spirits and teachings that come from demons.***

1 Timothy 1:4

Disregarding demons or developing an unhealthy interest and fear of them are both serious errors. In Ephesians 6, we see that we are at war against demons. We are to fight against our enemy, standing victorious and undefeated.

> ***Finally, my brothers, be strong in the Lord and in the power of His might. Put on the whole armor of God that you***

may be able to stand against the schemes of the devil. For our fight is not against flesh and blood, but against principalities, against powers, against the rulers of the darkness of this world, and against spiritual forces of evil in the heavenly places.

Ephesians 6:10-12

The scriptures show that Spirit-filled believers can compromise their protection and become filled with demons. In Acts 4, we read that all the believers were filled with the Holy Spirit.

When they had prayed, the place where they were assembled together was shaken. And they were all filled with the Holy Spirit and spoke the word of God with boldness.

Acts 4:31

Then, immediately afterward, we read that two of these Spirit-filled believers allowed Satan to fill their hearts. This means they had allowed the devil into their lives.

Now a man named Ananias, with his wife Sapphira, sold a piece of property. He kept back part of the proceeds with his wife's knowledge and brought a part of it and placed it at the apostles' feet. Then Peter said, "Ananias, why has Satan filled your heart to deceive

> ***the Holy Spirit and keep back part of the proceeds of the land?***

Acts 5:1-3

Ananias chose to sin, allowing Satan to gain a position in his life. The Holy Spirit doesn't leave us when we sin, but if we allow a demon into us, we have both the Holy Spirit and a demon dwelling in us. Many Christians today have this problem and are the most difficult people to deal with in ministry. The demons influence them, and they cause many issues among God's people.

Christians argue about whether a believer can have a demon or not, and those who do, disagree about how or where a demon can inhabit us. I do not want to get embroiled in such arguments because I do not see that they are profitable. The reality is that if we have a demon, we have a problem. It does not matter if we say a person is possessed, oppressed, or inhabited by demons. We need to find how the demons gained access to the person, close the doorway, and then expel the evil spirit.

I would say that the correct term to use would be to say that a person is demonized. This means that a demon is growing in influence in their life, and we need to intervene and put a stop to it. Demons can attack us from the outside, often tempting us to sin. Some classic examples of how demons operate would be that they first begin by throwing thoughts of fear into our minds. If we are not alert to the source and nature of these thoughts, we begin to feel fearful, and these feelings and thoughts start to increase if we are passive towards the demons attacking us. As we submit to the demons of fear, they begin to have a place in our lives, and their influence starts to grow. We become vulnerable to these spirits of fear because we disobeyed the scriptures and consequently lowered our defenses, becoming open to enemy attacks.

> ***For though we walk in the flesh, we do not war according to the flesh. For the weapons of our warfare are not carnal, but mighty through God to the pulling down of strongholds, casting down imaginations and every high thing that exalts itself against the knowledge of God, bringing every thought into captivity to the obedience of Christ.***

2 Corinthians 10:3-5

This passage commands us to be aware of and aggressive toward spiritual attacks. Demons usually start their attacks by throwing thoughts into our minds. Sin begins with a single thought. We are commanded to cast down imaginations and thoughts that disagree with God. Imaginations can be translated as arguments, or reasoned arguments. Why are we so passive and ignorant of the way the enemy operates? We should be schooled in the scriptures more. We must do as we are instructed and take all thoughts captive to the obedience of Christ. When Satan assaulted Jesus in the wilderness, He countered all the devil's arguments and reasonings with the Word of God.

> ***Then Jesus was led up into the wilderness by the Spirit to be tempted by the devil. And He had fasted for forty days and forty nights, and then He was hungry. And the tempter came to Him and said, "If You are the Son of God, command that these stones be turned into bread." But He answered,***

"It is written, 'Man shall not live by bread alone, but by every word that proceeds out of the mouth of God.]" Then the devil took Him up into the holy city and set Him on the highest point of the temple, and said to Him, "If You are the Son of God, throw Yourself down. For it is written, 'He shall give His angels charge concerning you,' and 'In their hands they shall lift you up, lest at any time you dash your foot against a stone.'" Jesus said to him, "It is also written, 'You shall not tempt the Lord your God.'" Again, the devil took Him up on a very high mountain and showed Him all the kingdoms of the world and their grandeur, and said to Him, "All these things I will give You if You will fall down and worship me." Then Jesus said to him, "Get away from here, Satan! For it is written, 'You shall worship the Lord your God, and Him only shall you serve.'" Then the devil left Him, and immediately angels came and ministered to Him.

Matthew 4:1-11

Demons rely upon us to be passive to the thoughts and feelings they throw at us. We must always be aggressive towards the enemy. Resist everything the devil throws at you! Whether it be sickness, thoughts, feelings, temptations, or circumstances.

When we have thoughts of fear, we need to take up our authority in Christ and tell fear to leave us in Jesus's name! If we suddenly start to feel depressed, or angry for no reason, or have impure thoughts flitting across our minds, then most likely we are coming under the attack from a demon. Do not buy into what the devil is offering you. Christians are often given a thought by the devil and then instantly own it as their own and run with it, like a runner in a relay race. We are offered the baton of sin, grasp it, and set off running. Instead of doing this, speak out loud to the fear, to the depression, lust, or wrong thoughts, and tell them to leave you at once in Jesus' name! Tell Satan to go, and to take his thoughts and feelings with him.

Demons rely upon us to be passive to the thoughts and feelings they throw at us.

> ***Therefore, submit yourselves to God. Resist the devil, and he will flee from you.***

James 4:7

Resist the devil. Do not tolerate negative words to be spoken over you either, even if they are from loved ones or well-meaning people.

Sickness was dealt with on the cross, so why do we allow a doctor to diagnose and declare a condition over us? If the doctor tells you that you will never recover from an illness, speak out loud and tell them that by the stripes of Jesus, I am healed! Refuse the sickness.

Resist lust and perverted thoughts. Go on the offensive against all such suggestions from the enemy. Resist the devil, and he will flee from you. One of the devil's most successful ploys is getting Christians to be ignorant of our authority over him. When a Christian tells a demon to leave, it has to go. We take up our authority in the name of Jesus and command demons to depart!

The devil is terrified of this knowledge getting out, and God's people stepping up to the plate, instead of acting like whipped curs and running scared of him. Resist him, and he will flee from us!

> ***God has not given us a spirit of fear, but of love, and power, and a sound mind.***

2 Timothy 1:7

Do you have thoughts of fear or anxiety? Thoughts that you are losing your mind and going mad? This contradicts scripture and needs to be broken in Jesus' name. We do not have a spirit of fear! We have the Holy Spirit living inside of us. We are not fearful people. We are bold, brave, courageous, and at peace. We have good mental health because Jesus has given us a sound mind. Speak this out loud over yourself. Do not allow negative thoughts or words from other people to say otherwise. You are healthy and stable, with a sound mind.

> ***I shall not die but live and declare the works of the Lord.***

Psalm 118:17

> ***With long life, I will satisfy him and show him My salvation.***

Psalm 91:16

God has a future and a hope for you. Satan wants to throttle your life and even end it prematurely if possible. God has said that you will live a long life, and you will be declaring the gospel. You will not die until you are satisfied with life. If you are not yet satisfied, then don't die! Resist all the devil wills for you, and don't listen to his lies, even for a second. Satan is a thief who comes to steal, kill, and destroy, but only if we passively allow him to do what he wants.

CASE STUDY TWO

I ministered to a woman who confessed to me that she was a lesbian and that I was the first person she had told. She said she wanted to "come out" to me because she trusted me as a minster of God and knew that I would still accept and love her. She said she had started to have thoughts of same-sex attraction several years earlier but had never acted on them. She said she could no longer deny her feelings and wanted to begin exploring lesbian relationships. I didn't know what to say, so I asked if I could pray for her. Immediately when I started praying, the Holy Spirit spoke to me and said that this was all a lie from the enemy. I stopped praying, looked at the woman, and said to her, "This is a lie. I break these thoughts in Jesus' name. You do not have same-sex attraction; the Lord says it is a lie from the enemy!" The woman looked startled, and instantly, all thoughts and feelings of same-sex attraction and the identity of being a lesbian departed. It was as though I had broken a spell over her. I told her to go and tell her family what had happened, which she did. Initially, her family was

The devil is terrified of this knowledge getting out, and God's people stepping up to the plate, instead of acting like whipped curs and running scared of him

devastated when she said these things, but they quickly understood that this was now no longer true. Several years have passed, and none of these wicked thoughts have ever returned to her. Today, she is a normal, healthy person, and those nasty thoughts are like an unpleasant dream fading away. Praise God!

OBSERVATIONS

Let us look at what was happening in the spirit realm in this situation. The woman said that some of her friends began to have same-sex attraction, with some declaring themselves bisexual, and others as lesbian. Around this time, she began to think that she was attracted to other women. She didn't like these thoughts and found them to be intrusive. She was worried about the consequences to her family of feeling attracted to women. She mistakenly believed these thoughts and feelings were from herself while actually they were being put into her mind by the demons around her. As she mixed with lesbians in her life, demons of homosexuality and perversion started to assault her. She wasn't alert to these spiritual attacks, and the demons continued to put feelings and thoughts into her. After several years of supposedly harboring the terrible secret that she was, in fact, a lesbian, she was coming to the point of accepting it. She felt she needed to start exploring her sexuality by declaring herself gay and finding a sexual partner. Suppose she had committed a sex act with a woman? In that case, the demons attacking her from the outside would have now been able to access her body and soul, and she would have become entirely overtaken by homosexuality.

Speak out loud.

This is a classic case study of how demons gain access to our lives. Fortunately, the Lord could use someone to speak a word that dispelled and exposed what the enemy was doing. His work was cast down, and all thoughts of same-sex attraction disappeared and have not returned! Praise God!

CONCLUSIONS

Demons tempt us to sin, and if we do so, we open ourselves up to the inflow of evil spirits. The only interest that demons have in sin is because it allows them to gain access to us. The devil does not want us to have a good time sexually. He uses sex as an easy route into our lives, and once he enters, he begins to cause havoc.

The good news is that Jesus died on the cross and rose to life again. The cross was a perfect work. Perfect in every respect, and perfect in every aspect. Jesus defeated Satan on the cross and regained the authority he stole from us in the Garden of Eden. Christians now have total authority over Satan and all demons. If you are tempted to sin, command the devil and his demons in Jesus's name to stop tempting you and leave you alone. Resist them. Insist that they leave you. Speak out loud. Be adamant and determined that they have to go in Jesus' name, and they will leave, and you will have the victory. The devil is reliant on people being passive and allowing him to do his nasty work in their lives. If we stand up to him, he has to leave and take his evil thoughts and feelings with him.

> ***Therefore, submit yourselves to God. Resist the devil, and he will flee from you.***

James 4:7

Sometimes, the demons will need to see that you are not going to give up and that you really mean what you are saying, and then when they see this, they will immediately depart. In James 4:7, it says that the devil will flee from us. He runs from us in the same way as a cat flees from a dog. Satan desperately scampers away. He will not stay around against a determined Christian who knows their authority and uses it against him. He knows the power we carry; he hangs around until he sees that we know what authority we have. Then he's out of here.

If you have sinned, the procedure is as simple and effective. Agree with the Lord that you have sinned. Apologize for doing so and commit to stop doing it. Then, take up your authority in the name of Jesus and command all demons that came into your life through the sin you committed to leave you at once in Jesus' name.

Again, the demons need to see that you mean what you say, know they have to go when you say so and that you are determined to stop doing the sin that allowed them to enter you in the first place. When demons see you are sincere and committed, they will leave immediately.

There is a simple procedure for these things. Sin allows the devil a place in your life. Confess the sin and stop doing it, and this denies the demons the right to be in your life. Next, use your authority and tell them that in the name of Jesus, they have to leave, and all the demons will go. We have the victory, the power, and the authority Jesus won for us at the cross. Satan quickly becomes discouraged around Christians who know what they are doing, and he doesn't stay long in their company.

CASE STUDY THREE

Another example is of a woman I knew. When she was a young Christian, she was single and wanted to be with a man.

One day, she met someone who liked her, but he wasn't a believer. She started dating him and soon began a sexual relationship with him. She knew it was wrong, but she would visit him in his flat and have sex with him; then, as she was leaving, she would say sorry to the Lord and then go about her way without a second thought. One day after visiting him, she was walking to her car, putting lip gloss on, and she said her usual prayer to the Lord, saying, "Lord, I know it's wrong, I'm sorry, and I ask You to forgive me," when the Lord spoke to her and said "I do not forgive you! You have written in your diary the time and day when you will come back to see him!" The woman realized that although she was confessing her sin, she had no intention of stopping doing it, as was evident by the entry she'd made in her diary. After thinking about things, she put the Lord first and stopped seeing the man. She now apologized to the Lord and could access God's forgiveness. She later became aware of the spiritual aspects of the sin and commanded all demons that had entered her to leave in Jesus' name.

CONCLUSIONS

We can see the spiritual dynamic at play in this case study. The woman was single and wanted to be married, but no suitor approached her. The devil began to put thoughts of lust and discontent into her, which she accepted as her own desires. She wasn't standing on scripture as she should have been and wasn't trusting in the Lord to provide a mate. The enemy then arranged for her to meet a man who wasn't a Christian and tempted her to go with him. Once she began having sex, she opened herself up to the inflow of demons of lust and fornication, and her relationship with the Lord started to suffer. The day came when the Lord got her attention and showed her the seriousness of her sin and the wrong choices she was making in life. She immediately repented and decided to stop doing it, and the devil started to lose power in her life. She later learned about taking authority over the demons that had entered her, commanding them to leave in Jesus' name. Her relationship with the Lord began to flourish again as she now spent time reading the Word and trusting the Lord as never before. Today, she is happily married to a fine Christian man.

The spirit realm works as one vast legal system. For example, if a demon temps us to sin sexually and we go on to break God's law, the protective wall around us is compromised, and the demon has the legal right to enter us. Conversely, when we confess that sin to God and turn from that sinful lifestyle, we benefit from His forgiveness. We now have claimed back the legal right to eject the demon out of us, and he has to go because he has lost the legal right to stay there.

In effect, we have taken back the legal right to authority in the situation by dealing with our sins. Once we have the legal right over the demon, it is simply a matter of ordering it to leave, and it has to go.

> ***If we confess our sins, He is faithful and just to forgive us our sins and to cleanse us from all unrighteousness.***

1 John 1:9

However, don't try casting demons out when you don't have the legal right to do so. Demons understand their rights and will refuse to leave if they have any legal grounds for staying. Usually, this is when the person refuses to acknowledge their sin or change their lifestyle. We cannot expect to dominate the devil while living in active sin. We are being double-minded, and the scriptures say that a double-minded man receives nothing from God.

> ***For let not that man suppose that he will receive anything from the Lord; he is a double-minded man, unstable in all his ways.***
>
> **James 1:7-8 NKJV**

Satan knows the Bible better than we do and will use it against us. The term "No Lord!" is a contradiction. If Jesus is our Lord, we follow Him and do what He says. When we fall into sin, we must quickly admit our mistake to God and stop doing it.

However, suppose we live a sinful lifestyle, such as an ongoing adulterous relationship, and categorically refuse to give it up. In that case, we are walking in rebellion to the Lord, and we become easy pickings for the devil. If we live in sin, we are inviting Satan and his demons into our lives, and we no longer have the legal right to cast demons out of us. This is why some deliverance sessions dissolve into long fights between manifesting demons and frustrated ministers.

Always deal with the person's sin and commitment to the Lord before deliverance. Demons understand their rights and will refuse to leave if they have any legal grounds for staying. Usually, this is when the person refuses to acknowledge their sin or change their lifestyle.

To confess means to make a clear, concise statement of fact. Charles Finney describes a detailed confession in his book 'Experiencing the Presence of God', page 208.

"Self-examination is looking at your life. It is considering your actions in the past and learning the true character of your life. Look over your personal history. Examine your personal sins one by one. I do not mean for you to glance at your past life, see that it has been full of sins, then go to God and make a general confession. That is not the way. You must look at your sins one by one. It is a good idea to look at your sins and take a pen and paper as you go over them and write each sin down as it occurs to you. Go over them as carefully as a merchant goes over his books. Each time a sin comes to mind, add it to the list. General confessions of sins will never do. Your sins have been committed one by one, and they should be repented of one by one."

The term "No Lord!" is a contradiction.

Review your life from birth to the present. Go over it more than once. Some sins allow demons the right to come into you but praise God, we can expel them in Jesus' name!

> ***whosoever shall call on the name of the Lord shall be delivered.***
>
> **Joel 2:32 KJV**

Demons can oppress us from the outside or inhabit us on the inside. In reality, if we have a demon, we have a problem, and Jesus commanded us to exercise the ministry of deliverance, which is to remove demons from people. We do this by speaking to them in the name of Jesus and commanding them to leave.

I recommend that all believers carefully examine their own lives and expel any demons present. We need to be prayerful and careful when casting demons out, and we need the guidance and help of the Holy Spirit.

Do not permit demons to manifest or speak at any time. Do not listen to anything they say, as demons are all liars. If we ask demons questions and receive information from them, we are sinning by being a medium, and if we are in active sin, it will make the deliverance session much more difficult. If they try to talk, command them to be silent and stop causing a disturbance. We must dominate the demons and order them to leave without making a show of themselves.

It is a good idea to work methodically when conducting a deliverance. It would help if you put some time aside to think through your life and write down all the incidents of sin you can remember. Do not show your lists to anyone; this is between you and the Lord. After the deliverance, you can burn the list.

Firstly, forgive anyone who has done you wrong, and ask God to bless them. Make a list of the sinful activities you have been involved with in life, and repent, which means you make a conscious decision never to do them again. List by name every person with whom you have sinned sexually. If you cannot remember the name, write down the incident. Also, write down other sinful sexual activities, such as pornography, sex with the same sex, sex with children, sex with animals, and sex with demons. Include any person you indulge in sexual fantasies with.

Sometimes, people have an image or a person they have sex with within their minds. These fantasies will begin to be controlled by demons and can also become a person you have sex with in your dreams when you are asleep. This is one of the ways people begin to have sex with demons.

Write down if you have been sexually molested and by whom, including rape or any sexual ritual. List each ritual separately. If you have been raped or molested, you did not sin, but the other person's sin allows demons to be placed into you and therefore needs to be listed and brought to the Lord so that you can be delivered from all demons in your life. The demonic agenda of ritualistic abuse, rape, and molestation is so that demons can be placed into you, and you can be controlled and used by demons to do their bidding.

We need to confess our sins, but we also need to deal with the spiritual consequences of these sins. The Church often misses the additional step of deliverance, but it is so important. You need to take authority over all demons that entered your life through these sinful activities and command them to leave you.

For example, if you had participated in homosexual acts with someone called Brenda, you would first confess to the Lord that you have sinned with Brenda and agree with the Lord that you sinned. The demons have now lost all rights to inhabit you, and it is a simple matter to command them to leave in Jesus' name.

You now speak out loud to the demons saying:

"All demons that came into my life through the sin of homosexuality with Brenda, I command you in Jesus' name to leave me at once and forever!"

Put some time aside to make your lists, and work through each incident or person, confessing sins and then commanding all demons that entered your life through those sins to leave, in Jesus' name. Write down all involvement with the occult, such as horoscopes, seances, fortune telling, watching horror movies, casting spells, meditation, and every practice of false religion. Listening to music that glorifies the devil, drunkenness, drug use, abortion, losing control of yourself with rages, accepting condemning or abusive words from others (which is the same as accepting a curse), and many other activities. The Holy Spirit will bring to your mind and convict you of the things you need to pray through, no matter how small or insignificant it may seem.

Sometimes, demons pass through the family line. If you suspect that this may be the case, tell the Lord about the sins that were committed by your forefathers and mothers, and ask the Lord to cleanse your family lines in Jesus' name. With each suspected area of your family where you think demons may be able to inhabit, ask the Lord to block any demons from continuing to travel through the mechanism of inheritance. Again, speak out loud and command all demons that pass through the generations to get out of you and leave your family forever. Ask the Lord to seal you and your immediate family from all demonic inheritance. See chapter 5 for more information on generational curses.

If we ask demons questions and receive information from them, we are sinning by being a medium.

Be prayerful and ask the Lord to show you how to pray and the areas of your life that have allowed demons to inhabit you. Take time to fast and seek the Lord, asking Him to give you discernment and a sensitivity to the Holy Spirit and His leading.

If you are in doubt about something, cast the demons out anyway. Suppose there are none there; no harm done. Be bold and adventurous. If in doubt, cast it out. Carefully go through your life and cleanse yourself of all demons. When you have finished, ask the Holy Spirit to fill you afresh. Please note, if we confess the sin but do not eject the demons that entered our lives through the sin, the demons will still be in us, and we will find it much harder to resist falling back into a sinful lifestyle. This is why many people backslide into sinful activities and don't have a long-term, consistently victorious Christian lifestyle.

AN EXAMPLE OF HOW TO CAST A DEMON OUT

Let us take an example of someone sinning by accessing pornography.

Prayer to pray, to be said out loud: -

"Lord Jesus, I confess to You that I am guilty of accessing porn. I repent of this activity and ask you to forgive me and cleanse me. Thank you, Jesus. Amen"

According to 1 John 1:9, you will now access God's total forgiveness into your life. The next step is to take authority over the demons of pornography, lust, and all other demons that entered you through this sin. Speak out loud, saying: -

"Demons of lust, demons of pornography, and every other demon that entered my life through the sin of accessing pornography, I take authority over you now in Jesus's name, and I command you to leave me and get out of my life right now in the name of Jesus's. Amen"

Speak out loud and use force! Speak with authority! When Jesus rebuked demons, the word rebuke could be translated as "Throttle!" You may have some images that seem to be burned onto your brain. Use the name of Jesus and smash those images, commanding them to disappear. You are now delivered from every demon that entered you through that sin. I want to stress that you can self-deliver privately, and nobody needs to know your sins. God wants to preserve your dignity and keep you safe. If you need support, ask a trusted and mature Christian to stand with you, but I advise you to do the commanding. Don't rely on someone else to speak to the demons; they need to understand that you mean it, that you are through with them, and that their time with you is over. Sometimes, the Holy Spirit will lead you to make lifestyle changes. In the case of pornography, it may help you to talk to a mature and trusted Christian about your sin. You may need to allow someone to monitor your phone or laptop, or even to get rid of these things for a while. Submit yourself to the Lord. Resist the devil, and he will flee from you! Be led by the Holy Spirit and remember that God loves and is with you every step of the way.

Those people who have engaged in homosexuality need to ask the Lord to literally re-create their minds to be healthy and wholesome again.

> ***For this reason God gave them up to dishonorable passions. Their women exchanged the natural function for what is against nature. Likewise the men, leaving the natural function of the woman, burned in their lust toward one another, men with men doing that which is shameful, and receiving in themselves the due penalty of their error. And since they did not see fit to acknowledge God, God gave them over to a debased mind, to do those things which are not proper. They were filled with all unrighteousness, sexual immorality, wickedness, covetousness, maliciousness.***

Romans 1:26-29

These verses from Romans state that in the case of homosexuality, the Lord has given the people over to a debased mind. This is a mind that has been damaged and perverted and has become deprived and evil. After deliverance, the person must ask the Lord to give them a new mind and restore their soul. Focusing on the Lord in worship and Bible study with constant Christian fellowship will significantly assist this healing process.

Delight yourself in the Lord, and He will give you the desires of your heart.

Psalm 37:4

By seeking the Lord and making Jesus the delight of your life, God will begin to place new desires into your heart and give you those new things you desire. This is how a homosexual can be healed, delivered, and re-made so that they begin to have healthy sexual desires and can be fulfilled in a lifestyle of heterosexual marriage and normality.

He leads me beside still waters. He restores my soul; He leads me in paths of righteousness for His name's sake.

Psalm 23:2-3

I also strongly recommend the extensive use of speaking in tongues to anyone coming out of homosexuality.

He who speaks in an unknown tongue edifies himself.

1 Corinthians 14:4

The word edify means to improve someone's mind. Speaking in tongues is essential in restoring your body, mind, and soul. Using this spiritual gift is essential when leaving lifestyles such as homosexuality, immorality, occult involvement, the practice of false religion, and in the recovery from assault and abuse.

Always prepare carefully when working in deliverance. Don't rely on a formular; be prayerful and allow the Holy Spirit to lead you. Don't be rushed. Prepare a safe place for the deliverance. Pray about where the deliverance is to take place. Make sure the building is sanctified and sealed and you know who is there. Choose a place where you won't be disturbed. We know that a demon has come out of a person when the legal ground has been reclaimed, and we command the demon to go in Jesus' name. There does not have to be any physical demonstration that a demon has come out. We cast demons out by FAITH, not by sight. That is why the issue of faith is so crucial in deliverance.

In Matthew 17:14-20 Jesus said this particular demon does not come out except by prayer and fasting. This doesn't mean we stop the deliverance session and go away and fast; it means that to build up our belief, we must have a lifestyle of prayer and fasting. In this passage, Jesus was talking about our belief in Him. Prayer and fasting build up our faith. It is often good to fast on the days leading up to a deliverance session, but on the day itself, it is best to eat. This is due to the intense spiritual warfare experienced during a deliverance. I recommend eating high-quality protein, such as red meat, with plenty of high-calorie foods to combat the physical tiredness and impact of spiritual warfare.

I also strongly recommend the extensive use of speaking in tongues to anyone coming out of homosexuality.

SUMMARY

- Forgive every person in your life unconditionally and let go of every offense.
- Study your Bible and ask the Lord to show you your sin.
- Confess your sin to the Lord and decide to stop doing it.
- Command all demons that entered you through each sin to leave at once in Jesus' name. Do this for each area of sin, not just a general prayer.
- Ask the Holy Spirit to fill you and help you to resist temptation.
- Read your Bible, pray, and speak in tongues daily to grow in the Lord.
- Join a strong church, commit to it, and become accountable to a trusted elder.

For further study on the subject of deliverance, I recommend the teachings of Derek Prince, Rebecca Brown MD, and John Ramirez.

Chapter Fifteen

DON'T LET YOUR PAST STEAL YOUR FUTURE

YOU HAVE A NEW IDENTITY FOR A NEW LIFE

as far as the east is from the west, so far has He removed our transgressions from us.

Psalm 103:12

Satan is constantly trying to separate us from the Lord. He uses guilt and shame to drive a wedge between us. God, however, is always there for us. No matter what has happened to us or what we have done. The Lord will never leave us, but we can turn away from Him, and we usually do this when we feel unworthy of Him. Do not allow the devil to build a wall between you and God. The devil tells us that we must put things right in life before we can return to the Lord, which is a total lie. God loves us as a Father, and we can bring our sins to Him because He wants to help us to straighten things out.

Satan is constantly attacking your relationship with Jesus and trying to redefine it. He wants you to see yourself as an employee of God rather than His child.

Imagine the relationship the owner of a large corporation has with his employees. His staff are simply people who work for him. As an employee, you may work hard and strive to do an excellent job for the company. You may do some training and progress into a management position, and if you serve faithfully with dedication, you may even become a board member. You will, however, only ever be an employee of the company. This is similar to how many Christians see themselves in God's eyes. They feel insignificant and unworthy, needing to serve the Lord faithfully even to be allowed to remain a part of His kingdom, never mind being able to have a close relationship with Him. This way of thinking is incorrect and is offensive to the Lord. You are not God's employee; you are His child. You don't need to make an appointment to see Him or feel that you must do all kinds of service and sacrifice to gain His favor. The act of sacrifice Jesus performed on the Cross qualifies you to be in God's family – not as an employee, but as His child. You have access to Him.

To go back to the analogy of the owner of the large corporation, an employee must show themselves to be an exemplary worker to be allowed to make an appointment to see the owner, and even then, it may not be granted to him. On the day of the meeting, the worker puts his best suit on, walks up the stairs to the head office, gives his name to the admin team, then takes a seat and waits to be seen. If the owner is busy or has forgotten about the meeting, they will have to come back another day and go through the whole process again. However, the owner's son or daughter can walk into the building and go straight to the owner's office without an appointment. Even if the owner is in an important meeting, He will always be delighted to see His child because He is doing all of it for them.

You are His child, He's always happy to see you, and you can walk in anytime, sit on your Father's knee, and talk to Him. He always has time for you because you are always on His mind. You are not just a face in a crowd. Your photo sits on His desk. You are why He is working so hard because He is preparing the company for you to inherit one day.

Jesus won the right for us to be children of God. We have access to Him because He is our Father. Jesus is the King of the kings, and you get to inherit His kingdom as one of His kings.

The devil tells us that we must put things right in life before we can return to the Lord, which is a total lie.

People sometimes think that God is so busy looking after the world that He doesn't have time for them. This is just a lie from the enemy. We serve an infinite God who has a one-on-one relationship with every one of His children all at the same time. The Lord isn't like us. God is so big, so incredible, and eternally infinite beyond our imagination, and we will never come to the end of Him. We will still be discovering new things about Him throughout all of eternity. We each get to have a personal relationship with the Lord, where we continually have His full attention, just as if we are the only person He relates to. It is a wonderful Father-son, or Daddy-daughter, special time with Him that He so enjoys and looks forward to. Never think you are just a face at the back of the crowd. Your Father is thinking about you continually every minute of every hour, every day of your life, and planning blessings and all good things for you. When we get to heaven, we will see these things in plain sight, but they are happening just the same here and now.

God loves you!!

He isn't angry with you.

You could never be good enough for him in your own strength, no matter what you did or didn't do, but your relationship is based on God's love and power, not on your performance.

God placed all the disapproval and condemnation you deserve onto Himself, His Son Jesus, on the Cross, so that you can become a part of the family!

God suffered the punishment you deserve. It was His blood that spilled onto the ground. It was His face that was disfigured. God Himself endured humiliation so that you don't have to.

God paid the penalty that you deserve. He experienced your guilt and shame because He wanted to provide forgiveness and friendship between you and Him.

Jesus died on the Cross so that you can be adopted into His family and have the status of being His child.

Benefits include the unconditional love of God your Father, forgiveness of all sin, healing from every sickness, and full inheritance rights. Jesus died on the Cross so that you could be written into God's will.

It doesn't matter what you have done.

God forgives you.

It doesn't matter how you have been degraded.

God accepts, restores, and honors you.

It doesn't matter how you feel about yourself; what matters is how God feels about you.

You may feel worthless, but God says, "My child! I love you, and you belong to Me!".

God isn't holding anything against you. He's not mad at you. He loves you and wants you as you are, sin and all.

All these blessings are yours.

Provided and paid for by the Cross.

Through the perfect work of the Cross, you are forgiven.

You are healed.

You are now a brand-new person.

You are validated.

You are legitimate.

You are accepted.

You are loved.

You are wanted.

You are His beloved child.

You are the apple of His eye.

Jesus will never leave you, so you will never be alone again.

And you have a place reserved for you in heaven.

God placed all the disapproval and condemnation you deserve onto Himself, His Son Jesus, on the Cross, so that you can become a part of the family!

Dealing with and letting go of guilt and shame is so empowering. Realizing your true identity in Christ will enable you to walk in the authority and destiny God has for you and gain victory over all that the devil throws at you.

Satan is desperately afraid of you discovering your true identity, so he is motivated to keep us disabled with shame, guilt, and low self-esteem.

Satan hates you, especially if you accepted Jesus as your Lord and Savior.

The devil hates you and is afraid of you because you are something he can never be.

You are a child of Almighty God.

Satan is consumed with jealousy and hatred towards you because of this.

Always remember that the devil is a loser who was sacked from his position in heaven.

He is illegitimate because he has no father, which means that Satan is a bastard.

He knows you can't be sacked like he was because you are family.

The devil wants you to believe that you're a shameful loser like himself.

Just remember, he's a lying bastard who has been forever humiliated and disgraced.

Satan is a loser. He suffered his final defeat when Jesus died on the Cross and then rose to life again. In his narcissistic, psychopathic rage, Satan attacks God's people by attempting to overwhelm them with shame, guilt, and feelings of rejection. The devil wants to weigh you down with low self-esteem and self-loathing.

He tempts you into sexual sin so he can then use it against you, making you feel guilty and ashamed. You can never seem to recover the cleanness and purity you lost. The more partners you have, the less valuable you feel, and the less significant your relationships become.

In addition to your sins, things may have been done to you, such as sexual assault and rape. These violations add to your sense of worthlessness, shame, and guilt, leaving you feeling stained and degraded.

There is only one answer to all this mess, and His name is Jesus.

Young people often suffer physical abuse and neglect, and many are sexually molested. Satan drives people to commit sexual abuse, especially against children, to break their hearts and destroy their ability to trust. Abuse allows the devil to put demons into people, and these evil spirits begin influencing them with thoughts and feelings of self-loathing, sexual perversion, bitterness, rebellion, and self-harm.

The devil hates children and gloats over their suffering. He intends to hurt them and shatter their self-image, leaving them feeling worthless, unloved, and unlovable, making them vulnerable to all he wants to do in their lives. A child who has been abused will often gravitate towards unsafe people who will continue to abuse them in life. Many homosexuals became so after suffering sexual molestation. Satan wants you to believe you are worthless, unloved, and unlovable. He wants you to become obsessed with yourself and unable to trust and love others as you should.

There is only one answer to all this mess, and His name is Jesus.

Jesus is the only one with the desire and the power to make you clean again. Jesus bore our guilt and shame on Himself at the Cross. He suffered for the wrong things that we have done. He suffered humiliation so we can leave our filth and brokenness at the Cross with Him.

We then receive the new life Jesus received when He rose from the dead. All our shame, guilt, and sin stay in the tomb with the Lord's grave clothes. We get to be born again with Him as a brand-new person. This is the greatest deal in the whole of history! Our salvation was very costly, but not for us. Jesus paid the price in full, and we can get it for free.

The crossroads of your life is when you decide to let go of your old self, of all that was done to you, your old identity, and all of the bad things you have done to others. You change direction and go forward into the rest of your life as a new person. The Cross is the place of death for your old self. You died with Him on the Cross, and because you were joined with Jesus in His death, you rose with Him to life as a brand-new person.

You are not a victim; you are a victor!

Mediate on scriptures and let the Word of God change how you feel about yourself. The Bible is medicine for your body and soul. The Word of God is the gateway to prosperity in every area of your life. Self-hatred and low self-esteem will hinder your progress, and you will find it difficult to break free from the old ways of living and receive the new things that God wants to bring into your life.

> ***Trust in the Lord with all your heart and lean not on your own understanding; in all your ways acknowledge Him, and He will direct your paths. Do not be wise in your own eyes; fear the Lord and depart from evil. It will be health to your body, and strength to your bones.***

Proverbs 3:5-8

God is trustworthy and safe. He is the only person who you can completely trust. You may have been the worst sinner in the world, or you may have suffered significant abuse from others, but God is able and willing to restore you completely. He will restore you to such an extent that it will be just as though you have never sinned or been abused in the first place.

> ***Come now, and let us reason together, says the Lord. Though your sins be as scarlet, they shall be as white as snow; though they be red like crimson, they shall be as wool.***
>
> **Isaiah 1:18**

When you choose Jesus as your Lord and Savior, you stop living as your old self, with the stains of this life covering you, and you live a new life, covered by the blood of Christ, which takes away ALL your sin and filth.

You are not a victim; you are a victor!

> ***Do you not know that the unrighteous will not inherit the kingdom of God? Do not be deceived. Neither the sexually immoral, nor idolaters, nor adulterers, nor male prostitutes, nor homosexuals, nor thieves, nor covetous, nor drunkards, nor revilers, nor extortioners will inherit the kingdom of God. Such were some of you. But you were washed, you were sanctified, and you were justified in the***

name of the Lord Jesus by the Spirit of our God.

1 Corinthians 6:9-11

God washes us spotlessly clean with Christ's blood, which is the most powerful detergent in the universe. To be sanctified means to be made holy. God's perfect work of the Cross is so powerful that you become as holy as Jesus is. When God looks at you, He sees you as pure, holy and perfect as His Son Jesus is. He justifies you. To be justified means it is just as though you had never sinned.

God does not condemn you.

God has forgiven you.

God restores you.

God renews you.

God gives you a future and a hope.

There are no second-class citizens in Christianity. We are ALL first class!

There is therefore now no condemnation for those who are in Christ Jesus, who walk not according to the flesh, but according to the Spirit.

Romans 8:1

When you became a Christian, God removed all condemnation from you. He placed all the punishment, rejection, disapproval, and condemnation you deserve on to Jesus at the Cross. By faith in Him, the shame, humiliation, and heartbreak that used to be yours was suffered by Jesus and dealt with by His death.

So let it all go.

Leave it behind and begin life again with your new self! Your old self died at the Cross, and your new self was born at the Cross. You were not saved by how good you are, but by how glorious Jesus is. A wicked person who gives their life to Jesus on their deathbed receives the same measure of salvation as the person who faithfully served the Lord all their life.

There are no second-class citizens in Christianity. We are ALL first class!

Satan will try to tell you that you still carry something of your old identity and reputation, that although you are a Christian, you will always be a second-class believer because of the terrible things that occurred in your old life. There is, however, no hierarchy in the Christian life. The only qualification we have is God's grace, which is sufficient for all our needs. The devil tries to categorize some Christians as more holy and worthy than others, but he is lying. The only hierarchy that exists is that we are above the devil.

Satan is below us! He was shamefully thrown out of heaven and forever disqualified. He was sacked from his job and rejected permanently by the Lord. Satan then suffered a total defeat at the Cross, where Jesus delivered a devastating and final humiliation. Satan is now under our feet, and we have authority over him. He is a defeated foe, humiliated, shamed, and rejected by God.

If ever Satan whispers to you that you aren't good enough for God, just remember that he is a lying bastard. Tell him where to go, and don't let his slimy lies linger in your ears.

My Jesus

You picked me up

From my desolation

Planted my feet

On solid ground

You are my candle in the darkness

My shelter from the storm

My rock shield and staff

You are the sword in my hand

You are my destination

You are my promised land

And now I can see clearly

Because on solid rock I stand

Lord I give myself to you

And everything that I do

'Cos I love you

Andrew Powell

Chapter Sixteen

RESTORATION AND HEALING

NOTHING IS WASTED

The Word of God heals and restores. When we turn to Christ and follow Him, we are so forgiven and restored that we can even preach to others about the very sins we have committed in life. When God forgives us, we are forgiven 100%. There are no second-class Christians. Do not let anyone look down on you or say that you need to prove yourself or work hard to earn your deliverance in any way.

I know of a man who had spent years in drug addiction and was saved and delivered miraculously. Immediately, the Lord spoke to him and told him to begin doing the work of an evangelist. The people in church rejoiced when he was saved but said that he wasn't ready to start evangelizing because he had just become a Christian and had just left his life of sin. They said he needed to spend time attending Bible classes and helping in the church. The man became discouraged and felt like the people didn't fully believe he had been delivered. Fortunately, the minister realized that he needed to allow the Holy Spirit to lead the situation, and he agreed for the man to start preaching the gospel. This man went out and started telling people about Jesus and what the Lord had done for him and began leading people to the Lord. He has worked for over 20 years now as a successful evangelist.

There is a false belief that once we have failed in a particular area, we can't preach to others, because to some degree we still carry the stain of sin, and it has become a part of our identity. This is not the case. Failing in life does not disqualify us from being able to tell others about their errors and telling them to repent. The restoration of the Lord is so complete that we can go out and tell others to stop sinning when they are committing the very sins in which we have just recently failed in. Jesus met the man with many demons in him in Mark 5, and after He had cast the devils out of him, the man became calm and in his right mind. Jesus sent him out to share with others what God had done for him, and the man went and preached about Jesus to all the towns nearby.

The restoration of the Lord is so complete that we can go out and tell others to stop sinning when they are committing the very sins in which we have just recently failed in.

> ***They came to Jesus and saw him who had been possessed with the legion of demons sitting and clothed and in his right mind. And they were afraid. Those who saw it told them how it befell him who had been possessed with the demons and also concerning the swine. Then they began to plead with Him to depart out of their region. When He entered the boat, he who had been possessed with the demons prayed Him that he might be with Him. Jesus did not let him, but said to him, "Go home to your friends and tell***

> ***them what great things the Lord has done for you and how He has had compassion on you." So he departed and began to proclaim in the Decapolis what great things Jesus had done for him. And everyone was amazed.***

Mark 5:15-20

I do not mean that if someone has only recently recovered from a sinful lifestyle, they can be thrust into leadership within the church. This is different; there must be a time of testing and consistency in their life before becoming a shepherd over God's people. But a sinner who has been forgiven is fully qualified to speak to others about their need to come to Christ and repent.

Let us look at the example of Peter. The Lord told Peter that he would fall into sin, but that afterwards he come back to the Lord and would be used to strengthen the other believers. Peter vowed never to deny Christ, then immediately fell into this sin.

> ***Then they arrested Him, and led Him away, and brought Him into the high priest's house. Peter followed at a distance. But when they had kindled a fire in the middle of the courtyard and sat down together, Peter sat among them. Then a servant girl saw him as he sat near the fire, and gazed at him, and said, "This man was with Him." <u>But he denied Him</u>, saying, "Woman, I do not know Him." A little later someone else saw him and said, "You also are one of them." Peter said,***

"Man, I am not!" About an hour later another man firmly declared, "Certainly, this man also was with Him, for he is a Galilean." Peter said, "Man, I do not know what you are saying." Immediately, while he was yet speaking, the rooster crowed. The Lord turned and looked at Peter. Then Peter remembered the word of the Lord, how He had told him, "Before the rooster crows, you will deny Me three times." And Peter went outside and wept bitterly. Peter fell into sin and denied three times that he even knew Jesus. Peter was crushed by his weakness and failings.

Luke 22:55-62 (underline mine)

So when they had eaten breakfast, Jesus said to Simon Peter, "Simon, son of John, do you love Me more than these?" He said to Him, "Yes, Lord. You know that I love You." He said to him, "Feed My lambs." He said to him again a second time, "Simon, son of John, do you love Me?" He said to Him, "Yes, Lord. You know that I love You." He said to him, "Tend My sheep." He said to him the third time, "Simon, son of John, do you love Me?" Peter was grieved because He asked him the third time, "Do you love Me?" He said to Him, "Lord, You know everything. You know that I love You."

> ***Jesus said to him, "Feed My sheep. Truly, truly I say to you, when you were young, you dressed yourself and walked where you desired. But when you are old, you will stretch out your hands, and another will dress you and carry you where you do not want to go." He said this, signifying by what kind of death he would glorify God. When He had said this, He said to him, "Follow Me."***
>
> **John 21:16-19 (underline mine)**

Jesus forgave Peter and spoke destiny over his life. The restoration work of God is so complete that it was just as though Peter had never sinned. He was qualified to preach to others even about the very sin he had recently committed because he had been forgiven and the slate wiped clean. A short while later, Peter addressed the people about their denial of Christ.

> ***When Peter saw it, he answered the people: "Men of Israel, why do you marvel at this man? Or why do you stare at us, as if by our own power or piety we had made him walk? The God of Abraham and Isaac and Jacob, the God of our fathers, has glorified His Son Jesus, whom you handed over and denied in the presence of Pilate, when he had decided to release Him. You denied the Holy and Righteous One and asked for a murderer to be granted to you, and you killed the Creator of***

Life, whom God has raised from the dead, of which we are witnesses. And His name, by faith in His name, has made this man strong, whom you see and know. And faith which comes through Him has given him perfect health in your presence.

Acts 3:12-16 (underline mine)

With accuracy and grace, Peter could pinpoint the people's sins, especially how they had denied Christ. Peter was without shame, fully restored, not because of his own goodness, but because he trusted in the finished work of the cross, knowing that he had received a full pardon and reinstatement, just as though he'd never sinned in the first place. This is a demonstration of the power of the cross. A person who accepts Jesus as their Lord and Savior is instantly forgiven and made into a saint. God often speaks amazing words of calling and destiny over recent converts, letting them know God has work for them to do. The apostle Paul is another example. The Lord spoke this over him at his conversion.

"For this man is a chosen vessel of Mine, to bear My name before the Gentiles and their kings, and before the sons of Israel. For I will show him how much he must suffer for My name's sake."

Acts 9:15-16

Although it was many years before he became an apostle, as soon as he became a Christian, he began to preach the good news about Jesus, and the Lord spoke destiny and ministry over him.

Stop evaluating Christians by what the world thinks about them or by what they seem to be like on the outside. Once I mistakenly thought of Christ that way, merely as a human being like myself. How differently I feel now! When someone becomes a Christian, he becomes a brand-new person inside. He is not the same anymore. A new life has begun! All these new things are from God who brought us back to himself through what Christ Jesus did. And God has given us the privilege of urging everyone to come into his favor and be reconciled to him. For God was in Christ, restoring the world to himself, no longer counting men's sins against them but blotting them out. This is the wonderful message he has given us to tell others. We are Christ's ambassadors. God is using us to speak to you: we beg you, as though Christ himself were here pleading with you, receive the love he offers you—be reconciled to God. For God took the sinless Christ and poured into him our sins. Then, in exchange, he poured God's goodness into us!

2 Corinthians 5:16-21 TLB

Mary Magdalene was another wonderful example of a person who overcame shame and guilt. She was known as having seven demons driven out of her, yet she became one of the Lord's most devoted and respected followers of Christ.

> ***Afterward, He went throughout every city and village, preaching and bringing the good news of the kingdom of God. With Him were the twelve and some women who had been healed of evil spirits and infirmities: Mary, called Magdalene, from whom seven demons had come out.***

Luke 8:1-2

Zacchaeus was a pathetic person with a bad reputation, but one meeting with the Lord changed him forever. You know when the Lord has genuinely touched someone, because the change in them isn't just in words, it goes right down to their pocket. The joy of salvation enabled Zacchaeus to change his relationship with money.

> ***But Zacchaeus stood and said to the Lord, "Look, Lord, I give half of my possessions to the poor. And if I have taken anything from anyone by false accusation, I will repay him four times as much." Jesus said to him, "Today salvation has come to this house, because he also is a son of Abraham. For the Son of Man has come to seek and to save that which was lost."***

Luke 19:8-10

If you are willing, the Lord will remove your sin and shame and make you into a glorious new person. God loves a challenge. The bigger the sin, the more glory Jesus wins for Himself as He transforms you.

CASE STUDY

I knew of a single young woman who became pregnant with an older man. When he discovered that she was with child, he left her. The woman went to church and confessed her sin, but the church she attended condemned her for having sex outside of marriage. Despite her sorrowful repentance, the church publicly punished her by making her sit in the back row of the church every week until the baby was born. This behavior from the church was displeasing to the Lord. What did they expect her to do? Have an abortion? She acknowledged that she had sinned. She needed help and encouragement, not some religious condemnation. Thankfully, she has been delivered from that congregation and thrives in a new church. Today, she has a beautiful daughter and is faithfully serving the Lord. When Jesus comes into your life, it is like the dawning of a new day. Everything He touched turns to gold.

> ***God loves to show us off and display us as His trophies. For all eternity, we will be seen as examples of His ability to turn worthless trash into perfection itself.***

- Homosexuals becoming cleansed and forgiven, re-made and freed from thoughts and feelings of same-sex attraction, married with a family.
- Former prostitutes getting married in church, dressed in white.
- The pornography user who is now cleansed and free from lust.
- Drug addicts and alcoholics clean and stable, helping others to get free.

But God is so rich in mercy, and he loved us so much, that even though we were dead because of our sins, he gave us life when he raised Christ from the dead. It is only by God's grace that you have been saved! For he raised us from the dead along with Christ and seated us with him in the heavenly realms because we are united with Christ Jesus. So God can point to us in all future ages as examples of the incredible wealth of his grace and kindness toward us, as shown in all he has done for us who are united with Christ Jesus. God saved you by his grace when you believed. And you can't take credit for this; it is a gift from God. Salvation is not a reward for the good things we have done, so none of us can boast about it. For we are God's masterpiece. He has created us anew in Christ Jesus, so we can do the good things he planned for us long ago.

Ephesians 2:4-10 NLT

God loves to show us off and display us as His trophies. For all eternity, we will be seen as examples of His ability to turn worthless trash into perfection itself. Glory to God! The provision for all of our needs is the cross. Jesus took our guilt, shame, and sin, so that by faith in Him, we no longer need to carry these burdens. Take time to meditate on the following scriptures. Read them slowly and think about them. Speak out loud to any thoughts or words said to you that were negative, including things you said about yourself. Say out loud, "Spirit of rejection and low self-esteem; I order you to leave me now in Jesus' name!"

Repeat this whenever you have bad thoughts about yourself, and you will start to feel different. Stand in front of the mirror each day, look at yourself, and say "Jesus loves you! Jesus wants you! God has good plans and a future for you! I can do whatever Jesus wants me to do today because He will enable me to do it! I AM HOLY!" Thank God continually for all that He has done for you. Shake off the lies of shame, guilt, rejection, and low self-esteem, and emerge as the person Jesus made you to be. You are not a face in the crowd. Our God is so wonderful. Jesus has a one-on-one relationship with each of His children continually. He can do this because He is not like us, He is an infinite God.

SCRIPTURES TO MEDITATE ON

> ***When someone becomes a Christian, he becomes a brand-new person inside. He is not the same anymore. A new life has begun!***
>
> **2 Corinthians 5:17 TLB**

> ***God has saved us and called us with a holy calling, not according to works, but according to His own purpose and grace, which was in Christ Jesus before time began.***
>
> **2 Timothy 1:9**

We are not worthless or insignificant. Even before He created the universe, God saw you in His mind's eye. You are not an accident or an afterthought. You were carefully selected out of millions of sperm to be given the precious gift of life, and you have the opportunity to live forever in heaven with the Lord. This is why we should never feel rejected, unwanted, or unloved. God is willing to fulfill the destiny spoken over you at conception. God chooses you according to His grace; it has nothing to do with how good you are or what has happened to you. God loves you, chooses you, and wants you. The Lord has called you with a holy calling to do His bidding in this world.

> ***For we are His workmanship, created in Christ Jesus for good works, which God prepared beforehand, so that we should walk in them.***

Ephesians 2:10

Each one of us is so precious and deeply loved by God Himself. The Lord created us in His image and gave each of us the gift of life and free will. The Lord is eagerly waiting for the day when you will decide to reach out to Him and accept His offer of adoption into His family as His beloved child.

> ***For I know the plans I have for you, says the Lord. They are plans for good and not for evil, to give you a future and a hope.***

Jeremiah 29:11 TLB

God gave this promise to a people who were in rebellion against Him. This is the nature of God, to speak Words of hope and life over each one of us, even the most desperately sinful person on the face of the earth. You may have been abused or committed terrible sins, but Jesus is bigger than all that. His power, love, and ability to save is bigger than your failures. Read and meditate on the following scriptures and allow God's thoughts about you to replace whatever ideas you may currently hold.

> ***The Lord your God is in your midst, a Mighty One, who will save. He will rejoice over you with gladness, He will renew you with His love, He will rejoice over you with singing.***
>
> **Zephaniah 3:17**

> ***Before I formed you in the womb, I knew you.***
>
> **Jerimiah 1:5**

> ***Consider how much love the Father has given to us, that we should be called children of God.***
>
> **1 John 3:1**

> ***Even if my father and mother abandon me, the Lord will hold me close.***
>
> **Psalm 27:10**

> ***But you are a chosen race, a royal priesthood, a holy nation, a people for God's own possession, so that you may declare the goodness of Him who has called you out of darkness into His marvelous light.***
>
> **1 Peter 2:9**

I can do all things because of Christ who strengthens me.

Philippians 4:13

Be strong and of a good courage. Fear not, nor be afraid of them, for the Lord your God, it is He who goes with you. He will not fail you, nor forsake you.

Deuteronomy 31:6

But God demonstrates His own love toward us, in that while we were yet sinners, Christ died for us.

Romans 5:8

For if our heart condemns us, God is greater than our heart and knows everything. Beloved, if our heart does not condemn us, then we have confidence before God. And whatever we ask, we will receive from Him,

1 John 3: 20-21

For God has not given us a spirit of fear, but of power and of love and of a sound mind.

2 Timothy 1:7 NKJV

Finally, my brothers, be strong in the Lord and in the power of His might.

Ephesians 6:10

And I will compensate you for the years the locusts have eaten - the larval locust, the hopper locust, and the fledging locust - My great army which I sent against you.

Joel 2:25

Bless the Lord, O my soul, and forget not all His benefits, who forgives all your iniquities, who heals all your diseases, who redeems your life from the pit, who crowns you with lovingkindness and tender mercies, who satisfies your mouth with good things, so that your youth is renewed like the eagle's.

Psalm 103:2-5

Come to Me, all you who labor and are heavily burdened, and I will give you rest.

Matthew 11:28

As far as the east is from the west, so far has He removed our transgressions from us.

Psalm 103:12

But the Lord is faithful, who will establish you and guard you from the evil one.

2 Thessalonians 3:3

O Lord, you have searched me and known me. You know when I sit down and when I get up; You understand my thought from far off. You search my path and my lying down and are aware of all my ways. For there is not a word on my tongue, but behold, O Lord, you know it fully. You put Yourself behind and before me and keep Your hand on me. Such knowledge is too wonderful for me; it is lofty, and I cannot fathom it. Where shall I go from Your spirit, or where shall I flee from Your presence? If I ascend to heaven, you are there; if I make my bed in Sheol, you are there. If I take the wings of the morning and dwell at the end of the sea, even there Your hand shall guide me, and your right hand shall take hold of me. If I say, "Surely the darkness shall cover me, and the light shall be as night about me," even the darkness is not dark to You, but the night shines as the day, for the darkness is like light to You. You brought my inner parts into being. You wove me in my mother's womb. I will praise you, for You made me with fear and wonder; marvelous are Your works, and You know me completely. My frame was not hidden from You when I was made in secret, and intricately put together in the lowest parts of the earth. Your eyes saw me unformed, yet in Your book all my days were written, before any of them came into being. How precious also are Your thoughts to me, O God, how great is the sum of them! If I should count them, they are more in number than the sand; when I awake, I am still with You.

Psalm 139:1-18

Chapter Seventeen

WHY HOMOSEXUALITY IS DIFFERENT FROM EATING SHRIMP

ISSUES REGARDING THE LAW OF MOSES

The Law was given to Moses and is recorded in the Bible in the books of Exodus, Leviticus, Numbers, and Deuteronomy. Some laws applied to the Israelites at that particular time, and some are moral laws that will stand forever. There were civil laws, such as dietary requirements, that were only specific to a period of time, and there were ceremonial laws, such as sacrificial requirements, that were fulfilled by the cross. Laws about food, clothing, sowing of crops, and animal sacrifices have expired, while moral laws such as the Ten Commandments and sexual laws will continue to apply for all time. The Mosaic Law applied to the people of Israel from the time of Moses to the cross of Christ. The Mosaic law can be divided into three categories: civil, ceremonial, and moral laws. I am not writing a book about the Pentateuch, but to explain, for example, why eating shellfish no longer applies but homosexuality is forbidden, I will take a brief look at these three groups and examine dietary laws, sacrificial laws, and laws of morality.

DIETARY LAWS

Before the Mosaic Law and after the cross, people were allowed to eat every kind of animal, but under the Mosaic time, from Moses to the Cross, certain foods were forbidden. Laws governing food were specific to Israel for a period of time only. God's commands regarding food were different before the Law and after the Cross. Before the Law, God commanded people to eat every animal. God told Noah that he could eat any animal he wanted to.

> ***Then God blessed Noah and his sons and said to them, "Be fruitful and multiply and fill the earth. Every beast of the earth and every bird of the sky and all that moves on the earth and all the fish of the sea will fear you and be terrified of you. They are given into your hand. Every moving thing that lives will be food for you. I give you everything, just as I gave you the green plant.***

Genesis 9:1-3 (Old Testament)

Also, after the cross, dietary food laws no longer applied because they were time-specific, and the laws governing them had expired.

> ***Therefore let no one judge you regarding food, or drink, or in respect of a holy day or new moon or sabbath days. These are shadows of things to come, but the substance belongs to Christ.***

Colossians 2:16-17 (New Testament)

> ***About noon the following day as they were on their journey and approaching the city, Peter went up on the roof to pray. He became hungry and wanted something to eat, and while the meal was being prepared, he fell into a trance. He saw heaven opened and something like a large sheet being let down to earth by its four corners. It contained all kinds of four-footed animals, as well as reptiles and birds. Then a voice told him, "Get up, Peter. Kill and eat." "Surely not, Lord!" Peter replied. "I have never eaten anything impure or unclean." The voice spoke to him a second time, "Do not call anything impure that God has made clean."***

Acts 10:9-15 (New Testament)

After the Cross, eating all kinds of animals was once again commanded by the Lord as something good and acceptable to Him.

> ***Eat whatever is sold in the meat market, asking no question for the sake of conscience, for "The earth is the Lord's, and everything in it. If any of those who do not believe invite you to a feast, and you desire to go, eat whatever is set before you, asking no question for the sake of conscience.***

1 Corinthians 10:25-27 (New Testament)

This passage shows that even if a gentile unbeliever invites you to a meal, you are to eat whatever is set before you. This will include foods that were forbidden under the law of Moses. However, the eating of the blood was a moral law; it was not time-specific to just apply under Mosaic law. Eating of blood is forbidden throughout the Bible.

> ***Only you shall not eat flesh with its life, that is, its blood.***

Genesis 9:4 (Old Testament)

After the Great Flood, the Lord told Noah that people could eat animals as well as plants, but they must not eat the blood. Therefore, animals had to be killed, and the blood drained before eating. This is why killing an animal by strangulation is forbidden. The blood will still be inside it when it is eaten.

> ***For the life of every creature is its blood; in its blood is its life. Therefore I said to the children of Israel: You shall not eat the blood of any creature, for the life of every creature is its blood.***

Leviticus 17:14 (Old Testament)

The New Testament continues to state that eating blood is wrong. Eating blood and sexual immorality are moral laws, not just Mosaic laws. The passage from Acts explains that believers in Christ are not to consider themselves under the time-specific Mosaic law, but they still need to observe the perpetual moral laws of abstaining from sexual immorality and not eating the blood of an animal.

> ***"Therefore my judgment is that we should not trouble those of the Gentiles who are turning to God, but that we***

write to them to abstain from food offered to idols, from sexual immorality, from strangled animals, and from blood. For Moses has had in every city since early generations those who preach him, being read in the synagogues every Sabbath." Then it pleased the apostles and the elders, with the whole church, to send chosen men from among them to Antioch with Paul and Barnabas, namely, Judas called Barsabas, and Silas, leading men among the brothers. They wrote this letter by their hand: The apostles and the elders and the brothers, To the brothers who are of the Gentiles in Antioch and Syria and Cilicia: Greetings. Since we have heard that some of us, whom we did not commission, have gone out and have troubled you with words, unsettling your minds, saying, "You must be circumcised and keep the law," it seemed good to us, being assembled in unity, to send chosen men to you with our beloved Barnabas and Paul, men who have risked their lives for the name of our Lord Jesus Christ. Therefore we have sent Judas and Silas, who will also speak to you, saying the same things. For it seemed good to the Holy Spirit and to us to put on you no greater burden than these necessary things: Abstain from food offered to idols, from

sexual immorality, from strangled animals, and from blood. If you keep yourselves from these, you will do well. Farewell.

Acts 15:19-29 (New Testament)

SACRIFICIAL LAWS

Jesus fulfilled the sacrificial laws forever when He offered Himself as a perfect sacrifice on the cross. Therefore, we no longer need to offer the blood of animals as an exchange for the punishment we deserve. Christ died on our behalf so that everyone can receive the gift of salvation through Him.

Every priest stands daily at his service, offering repeatedly the same sacrifices, which can never take away sins. But when Christ had offered for all time a single sacrifice for sins, he sat down at the right hand of God.

Hebrews 10:11-12 (New Testament)

Christ has redeemed us from the curse of the law by being made a curse for us.

Galatians 3:13 (New Testament)

The Mosaic law of offering sacrifices was completed once and for all time by Jesus on the cross.

LAWS OF MORALITY

Homosexuality and all sexual sin have consistently been forbidden throughout the Bible, as was murdering your children for your prosperity or convenience. Homosexuality and child sacrifice will always be an abomination to a Holy God. Before the Mosaic Law, God destroyed the world with the Great Flood because of such sins.

> ***You may dismiss the stories in the Bible as fairy tales, but to say that the text does not condemn homosexuality is, at best, inaccurate and at worst, a deliberate falsehood.***

> ***The Lord saw that the wickedness of man was great on the earth, and that every intent of the thoughts of his heart was continually only evil. The Lord was sorry that He had made man on the earth, and it grieved Him in His heart. So the Lord said, "I will destroy man, whom I have created, from the face of the earth—both man and beast, and the creeping things, and the birds of the sky, for I am sorry that I have made them." But Noah found grace in the eyes of the Lord.***

Genesis 6:5-8 (Old Testament)

Before the law was given to Moses, there was a culture of homosexuality in the cities of Sodom and Gomorrah, and God destroyed them because their sin had become so great. This destruction of Sodom and Gomorrah exemplifies how serious God considers homosexuality to be and serves as a warning of the coming judgment that awaits those who flaunt

God's ways with sexual sins. This condemnation of homosexuality was recorded in Genesis 19 and referred to in the New Testament book of Jude. I include other scriptures from both the Old and New Testaments.

> ***But before they retired for the night, all the men of Sodom, young and old, came from all over the city and surrounded the house. They shouted to Lot, "Where are the men who came to spend the night with you? Bring them out to us so we can have sex with them!"***

Genesis 19:4-5 NLT (Old Testament)

> ***And don't forget the cities of Sodom and Gomorrah and their neighboring towns, all full of lust of every kind, including lust of men for other men. Those cities were destroyed by fire and continue to be a warning to us that there is a hell in which sinners are punished.***

Jude 1:7 TLB (New Testament)

> ***Do not practice homosexuality, having sex with another man as with a woman. It is a detestable sin.***

Leviticus 18:22 NLT (Old Testament)

Do you not know that the unrighteous will not inherit the kingdom of God? Do not be deceived. Neither the sexually immoral, nor idolaters, nor adulterers, nor male prostitutes, nor homosexuals.

1 Corinthians 6:9 (New Testament)

The wrath of God is revealed from heaven against all ungodliness and unrighteousness of men, who suppress the truth through unrighteousness. Therefore God gave them up to uncleanness through the lusts of their hearts, to dishonor their own bodies among themselves. They turned the truth of God into a lie and worshipped and served the creature rather than the Creator, who is blessed forever. Amen. For this reason God gave them up to dishonorable passions. Their women exchanged the natural function for what is against nature. Likewise the men, leaving the natural function of the woman, burned in their lust toward one another, men with men doing that which is shameful, and receiving in themselves the due penalty of their error. And since they did not see fit to acknowledge God, God gave them over to a debased mind, to do those things which are not proper.

Romans 1:18 and 24-28 (New Testament)

Homosexuality is consistently forbidden in both the Old and New Testaments of the Bible.

You may dismiss the stories in the Bible as fairy tales, but to say that the text does not condemn homosexuality is, at best, inaccurate and at worst, a deliberate falsehood.

Chapter Eighteen

GOD WILL HONOUR THE DECISIONS YOU MAKE

WE GET TO CHOOSE WHERE WE SPEND ETERNITY

Seek the Lord while He may be found, call you upon Him while He is near. Let the wicked forsake his way, and the unrighteous man his thoughts. and let him return to the Lord, and He will have mercy upon him, and to our God, for He will abundantly pardon.

Isaiah 55:6-7

Jesus made a comparison between two people. One who submitted to God's ways and the other who rejected His council. He said they were like two house builders, one who built on a solid rock foundation and the other on sand. A storm visited both houses. The first one was unmoved, while the second one collapsed.

"Not everyone who says to Me, 'Lord, Lord,' shall enter the kingdom of heaven, but he who does the will of My Father in heaven. Many will say to Me in that day, 'Lord, Lord, have we not

prophesied in Your name, cast out demons in Your name, and done many wonders in Your name?' And then I will declare to them, 'I never knew you; depart from Me, you who practice lawlessness! "Therefore, whoever hears these sayings of Mine, and does them, I will liken him to a wise man who built his house on the rock: and the rain descended, the floods came, and the winds blew and beat on that house; and it did not fall, for it was founded on the rock. "But everyone who hears these sayings of Mine, and does not do them, will be like a foolish man who built his house on the sand: and the rain descended, the floods came, and the winds blew and beat on that house; and it fell. And great was its fall."

Matthew 7:21-28

God gave us the precious gift of life, and we can choose whether to follow Him or go another way. A storm is coming upon the world. Battle lines are drawn up, and the day of decision is here. Very soon, our lives will be over, and we will all give an account before God and face the consequences of our choices. Those who accepted Jesus as their Lord and Savior will enter heaven to be with Him forever, while those who rejected Jesus will be thrown into the everlasting flames of Hell. Choosing Jesus means agreeing with Him on all matters and doing what He says. If you make a mistake, He forgives you every time and gives you a fresh start. If you stubbornly live an unrepentant lifestyle in rebellion against

Jesus, then He is not your Lord. You are living in opposition to Him and His kingdom.

> ***Be not deceived. God is not mocked. For whatever a man sows, that will he also reap. For the one who sows to his own flesh will from the flesh reap corruption, but the one who sows to the Spirit will from the Spirit reap eternal life.***

Galatians 6:7-8

Either we are for Jesus, or we are against Him. No one gets to abstain or sit on the fence. Not choosing Jesus in any way is an active choice against Him.

> ***(Jesus said) "He who is not with Me is against Me, and he who does not gather with Me scatters."***

Luke 11:23

Those who follow Him will continue to be with Him when they leave this life, while those who do not choose Jesus are separated from Him according to the decision they have made, and this separation continues after they die. Hell is a real place and the ultimate horror story. The consequences of going there are beyond catastrophic.

When you die, you will be given a new body that will endure for all eternity. It will never wear out, break down, or cease to exist. You will live forever in Heaven with Jesus, or you will live forever in Hell.

In Hell, there is no rest, no sleep, no water, no comfort, no companionship, no respite, no hope, and no ending. You will continue to suffer night and day in isolation from others. You will be in such agony that your earthly body would die within seconds, but your new body will be able to suffer the agony but be unable to die. There is no love there. Nobody to comfort you. Your body will burn continually, and your desperate screams will go unanswered. You will be tormented with the full recollection of your life on earth and the dreadful consequences of your decision to reject Jesus as your Lord and Savior. You need to humble yourself now while you still have the opportunity to do so.

Not choosing Jesus in any way is an active choice against Him.

Hell is a real place!

Jesus had a great deal to say about hell. Why is Jesus called the Savior? What did He come to save us from? Jesus came to save us from hell. He loves you and was prepared to do ANYTHING to keep you from going there. Even to suffer the indignity of being born into this world and dying on the cross. God does not take responsibility for you going to hell. He gave you free will, and He will honor your life choices. Your decisions in this life will determine whether you spend eternity in heaven or hell.

> ***Do not fear those who kill the body but are not able to kill the soul. But rather fear Him who is able to destroy both soul and body in hell.***

Matthew 10:28

"Enter at the narrow gate, for wide is the gate and broad is the way that leads to destruction, and there are many who are going through it, because small is the gate and narrow is the way which leads to life, and there are few who find it.

Matthew 7:13-14

Hell is a real place!

I urge you to read the words of Jesus in the gospels. God has only love and compassion towards everyone who is lost in homosexuality or other sinful activity. Jesus had so much to say about hell, and He has done everything He can to prevent you going there.

But God showed his great love for us by sending Christ to die for us while we were still sinners.

Romans 5:8 TLB

While you are still in sin, Jesus loves you and offers you the free gift of forgiveness and a brand-new start in life.

"Truly, truly I say to you, whoever hears My word and believes in Him who sent Me has eternal life and shall not come into condemnation but has passed from death into life."

John 5:24

God does not want anyone to continue in sin or end up in hell. He wants to help you and set you free. Christians must not be judgmental towards homosexuals, but we must tell them that God loves them and has the power to forgive, cleanse, and restore them from all that has perverted and distorted them. You get to choose whom you will follow, whom you will serve, and with whom you will spend eternity.

Jesus came to save us from hell. He loves you and was prepared to do ANYTHING to keep you from going there.

The choice is yours.

Chapter Nineteen

HOW TO BECOME A CHRISTIAN

A NEW BEGINNING

If you have never asked Jesus to be your Lord and Savior, you can do this now. If you mean what you say, then God is faithful and will forgive you of all your sins, and He will come and live in your heart. Consider this Bible verse and then pray the prayer, knowing that God is listening and will grant you your request.

> ***If we confess our sins, he is faithful and just to forgive us our sins, and to cleanse us from all unrighteousness.***
>
> **1 John 1:9 KJV**

PRAYER TO PRAY

Lord Jesus Christ, Almighty God, I believe in You and acknowledge that You are Lord.

I confess that I am a sinner before You. You are right and I am wrong. I humbly submit to Your Word, the Bible, as the final authority on all matters. Please forgive me of all my sin. Thank you that Jesus that you came and died for me on the cross, then rose to life again. I now gladly receive the forgiveness of sins that Jesus won for me on the cross. I ask You to fill me now with your Holy Spirit. Thank you for this forgiveness, for Your Holy Spirt and for the gift of eternal life. I ask all this in the name of Jesus. Amen

> ***Listen! I stand at the door and knock; if any hear my voice and open the door, I will come into their house and eat with them, and they will eat with me.***

Revelation 3:20 GNT

Now ask God to baptize you with His Holy Spirit.

PRAYER TO PRAY

Heavenly Father, thank you for forgiving me of all my sins and coming to make your home in my heart. I ask You now to completely baptize me with Your Holy Spirit, and to give me the gift of speaking in tongues. Thank you, Jesus! Amen

> ***Follow after love and desire spiritual gifts, but especially that you may prophesy.***

1 Corinthians 14:1

PRAYER TO PRAY

Heavenly Father, I thank You for baptizing me with Your Holy Spirit. I ask you to release gifts of the Holy Spirit into my life, of prophecy, discernment, knowledge, tongues, wisdom, helps, faith, encouragements, healings, and all that you have for me. Thank you, I receive these things in Jesus name. Amen

Printed in Great Britain
by Amazon

45480530R00136